Belgium: Entrance to Beguinage in Bruges

Major Cities of Europe

LITTLE HILLS PRESS

© Little Hills Press, **July 1997**
Photographs: see Publisher.
© Inside back cover: Duggan Co-operative.
Cover by NB Design
Maps: MAPgraphics
Printed in Hong Kong

ISBN 1 86315 107 9

Produced by Fay Smith and LHP editorial staff.
UK and Ireland written by Joan Beard.

Little Hills Press
Regent House
37-43 Alexander Street
Crows Nest NSW 2065 Australia

DISCLAIMER

Whilst all care has been taken by the publisher and authors to ensure that the information is accurate and up to date, the publisher does not take responsibility for the information published herein. The recommendations are those of the author, and as things get better or worse, places close and others open, some elements in the book may be inaccurate when you get there. Please write and tell us about it so we can update in subsequent editions.

Front Cover: A section of the square in the old town part of Frankfurt/Main opposite *the Romer*.

Back Cover: The Vatican.

Contents

❑ ❑ ❑ ❑

Austria

Land-locked Austria is situated in Central Europe and has an area of 83,849 sq km. It is a democratic federal republic of nine provinces, with a total population of 7,896,000. The capital is Vienna, where approximately a fifth of the population live, and the language of the country is German.

Austria is very mountainous with peaks reaching up to 3800m. It is a popular skiing venue with snow from January to the end of April in some parts.

Climate

Austria has a moderate climate, temperatures varying according to altitude. Generally winter extends from December to March, and average temperatures are 19C in July and -2C in January.

Entry Regulations

Visitors must have a valid passport, but a visa is not required for visits up to three months (six months for holders of British passports).

The duty free allowance is 400 cigarettes or 100 cigars or 500 grams of tobacco, 2 litres of wine and 1 litre of spirits. There is no restriction on the import or export of foreign currencies, but export of local currency must not exceed AS15,000. No vaccinations are required for any international traveller.

Currency

The currency of the land is the Austrian Schilling (AS), which is divided into 100 Groschen. Approximate exchange rates, which should be used as a guide only, are:

A$	= 7.20AS
Can$	= 6.90AS

NZ$	= 6.30AS
S$	= 7.00AS
UK£	= 15.50AS
US$	= 9.70AS

Notes are in denominations of 5000, 1000, 500, 100, 50 and 20 Schillings, and coins are 500, 100, 50, 25, 20, 10, 5 and 1 Schillings, and 50, 10, 5 and 2 Groschen.

Banks are generally open 8am-12.30pm, 1.30-3pm Mon, Tues, Wed and Fri, 8am-12.30pm, 1.30-5.30pm Thurs. All banks are closed Sat and Sun. Exchange counters at airports and the main railway stations are usually open 8am-10pm daily.

Shopping hours are 8am-6.30pm Mon-Fri, 8am-1pm Sat except for the first Sat of the month when they stay open until 5pm. Many shops close for two hours in the middle of the day.

Credit cards are widely accepted in the major cities, but not in the smaller towns even at petrol stations.

Telephone

International direct dialling is available and the International code is 00, the country code 43. The area code for Vienna is 01 or 09, that for Salzburg is 0662. Payphones have slots that take 1, 5, 10 and 20 schilling coins, and an audible tone warns that time is running out.

It is expensive to make international calls from hotels.

Driving

An International Driving Licence is necessary to hire a car, and third party insurance is obligatory. It is compulsory to wear a seat-belt, and children under 12 years of age are not permitted in front seats. Speed Limits are:

Cars:

built-up areas	50kph,
open roads	100kph,
motorways	130kph;

With Trailer under 750kg -

open roads	100kph,
motorways	100kph;

With Trailer over 750kg -

open roads	80kph,
motorways	100kph.

DETAIL OF THE PUBLIC TRANSPORT SYSTEM OF VIENNA

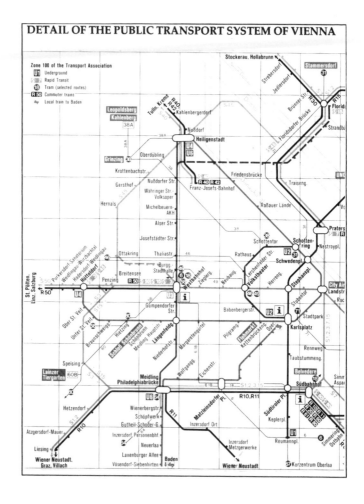

You should expect to pay tolls on many of the road tunnels and mountain roads.

Miscellaneous

Local time is GMT + 1 (Central European Time) with daylight saving in force from late March to late September.

Electricity - 220v AC, with round, two-pin plugs.

Health - Austria has good health services but they are very expensive. It is recommended that visitors have adequate medical insurance.

Vienna

Gateway to eastern Europe and capital of Austria, Vienna (Wien) lies on the banks of the Danube, near the borders of Hungary, Slovakia and Czechia.

It is very much a city of music, having been home to such composers as Mozart, Bruckner, Beethoven, Schubert, Brahms, Haydn and Johann Strauss.

History

The site of Vienna was occupied by the Celts long before the birth of Christ, and it was known to have been a Roman military camp called Vindobona in the year 1AD.

In 1155, the Babenbergs, the first dynasty to reign over Austria, chose Vienna as their residence. During the reigns of Leopold V and Leopold VI, the city underwent considerable expansion, financed in part by the ransom the English were forced to pay the Babenbergs for the return of their captured King Richard the Lionheart.

Rudolf I of Hapsburg took control of Austria after victory in the Battle of Durnkrut in 1278, but the people were not too thrilled about him and subsequently rebelled. However, it is the Hapsburgs that Vienna has to thank for her reputation as one of the great cities of the world - particularly Charles VI and Maria Theresia in the 18th century and Francis Joseph in the 19th.

Tourist Information

Tourist information offices are located at 38 Karntner Strasse (Opera House), and 40 Obere Augarten Strasse, ph (01) 211 140.

Local Transport

Vienna has an excellent public transport system. The U-Bahn (underground railway) has three lines, and there are bus, trolley and rail services to all parts of the city.

For an interesting way to visit the old parts of the city, hire a fiaker and listen to the driver's tales of Viennese life in olden days. Allow plenty of time.

Accommodation

Plaza Hilton, a deluxe hotel in the downtown area. Facilities include restaurants, bars, coffee shop, health club and shops.

Scandic Crown, is a superior first class hotel in the midtown area. Facilities include restaurants, bars, coffee shop, health club, swimming pool, tennis court and shops.

Park Schoenbrunn, a first class hotel in the midtown area. Facilities include restaurants, bars, coffee shop, health club, swimming pool, shops and a beauty salon.

There are six youth hostels in Vienna:

Jugendgasterhaus Wien Brigittenau, Friedrich Engelsplatz 24, ph (1) 330 0598, fax (1) 330 8379.

Jugendherberge Wien, Myrthengasse 7, Neustiftgasse 85, ph (1) 523 6316, fax (1) 523 5849.

Jugendherberg Lechnerstrasse, Lechnerstrasse 12, ph (1) 713 1494.

Hostel Ruthensteiner, Robert Hameringgasse 24, ph (1) 893 4202.

Jugendgastehaus der Stadt, Schlossberggasse 8, ph (1) 877 1501, fax (1) 877 0263.

Schlossherberge am Wilhelminenberg, Savoyenstrasse 2, ph (1) 458 5037.

Food and Drink

The most famous dish from this city is Wiener Schnitzel, but there are many more national dishes to tempt the taste buds, including various types of sausage.

In the suburbs of Grinzing, Sioevering, Heiligenstadt and Nussdorf, a cluster of fir twigs hanging above the door of an inn means that the year's wine is ready to be enjoyed. These are known as Heurigen localities, and the wine can only be from the innkeeper's own vineyards. There is also Heurigen music to accompany the wine and food, and it usually consists of a quartet of two violins, an accordion and a guitar, who play traditional Schrammel tunes. It is great fun, and very popular with the locals.

Sightseeing

Walking Tour
The Ring is an avenue that was created after the city wall was removed in 1857. It has several names as it circles the old city - Schotten Ring, Dr Karl Lueger Ring, Dr Karl Renner Ring, etc.
The **Stock Exchange** is on Schotten Ring, and to the south are the main buildings of the **University**, the new Gothic **Rathaus** (Town Hall - guided tours available), and opposite is the famous **Burg Theatre** (Palace Theatre - guided tours available).
To the south is the much-loved **Volksgarten** (people's gardens) with the **Theseus Temple**. On the other side of the Ring is **Parliament House**, which is built like a Greek temple. In front of the building is a monumental fountain topped by a 14m statue of Pallas Athene, and the poles on each side of the fountain fly flags when parliament is sitting. When there are no flags guided tours are available. It is a very photogenic building. Next are the **Alte Hofburg** and the **Neue Hofburg** (Old and New Imperial Palaces) on Helden Platz, the seat of the Hapsburg family and centre of a world empire.
Nowadays they are open to the public and contain the **National Library** and the **Ethnological Museum**.
In Michaeler Platz, in the direction of the city, is the **Looshaus** and unsurpassed views of the sprawling Old Hofburg. Also in the Hofburg is the world famous **Spanish Riding School** whose Lipizzaner horses have morning work-outs Sept-Dec, and tickets are available at the entrance. At the end of the Hofburg is the **Albertina** which houses the world's largest collection of graphic arts. Near here in Philharmoniker Strasse is the famous Hotel Sacher which sells the original Sacher's Torte.

Turn left and walk along Neuer Markt to the **Kapuziner Church** and the **Hapsburg Crypt**, which contains the sarcophagi of 137 members of the royal family, including twelve emperors and sixteen empresses. The tomb of the beloved Maria Theresia is considered by some to be one of the most beautiful examples of rococo art.

Go through the **Burgtor** (gate) and cross the Ring to the **Natural History** and **Fine Arts Museums**, both of which started off with the emperors' collections. In the middle of the park between the two buildings is the **Maria Theresia** memorial. Along the Opern Ring behind the New Hofburg are the Hofburg Gardens which have many memorials: Emperor Franz Joseph, Mozart, Goethe and others.

From here it is just a short walk to the **Opera House**, the first of the monumental buildings erected on the Ring. Although it is very much the centre of cultural life in Vienna, it was not well received either during its construction or upon its completion. Built in the French Renaissance style, people likened it to a railway station and made other derogatory statements to the point where one of the architects committed suicide. The opera house opened on May 25, 1869, with a presentation of Mozart's *Don Giovanni*. Guided tours are available.

Following Karntner Strasse from the Opera House towards St Stephan's Cathedral, the main shopping area is on the left, and it stretches past Neuer Markt to Kohl-markt. The streets here are -3pedestrian malls, and contain a wide variety of shops from up-market boutiques to souvenir stalls. There are also many coffee shops and-2 restaurants.

St Stephan's Cathedral was originally consecrated in 1147, and was a Romanesque structure. The Gothic reconstruction commenced in 1304, and was consecrated 36 years later. At the end of the 16th century a Renaissance-style octagonal capped roof and a belfry were added. It is one of the great churches of Europe and well worth a visit.

Sights Further Afield

The **Belvedere Palace** is situated on a rise south of the city centre. It was built for Prince Eugene of Savoy at the beginning of the 18th century, and is a masterpiece of sophisticated Baroque architecture. Prince Eugene played a major part in Vienna's liberation from the Turks, and consequently became very popular with the Emperor and the local people. The Emperor had the Belvedere built in gratitude, and the local people made sure the Prince kept control of the army when he was threatened with dismissal.

The State Treaty releasing Austria from its 10 years of occupation was signed in the Belvedere Palace on May 15, 1955. The upper belvedere can be reached from Prinz Eugen Strasse and the Gurtel, and it has a gallery of 19th and 20th century paintings, including works by Gustav Klimt and Egon Schiele. The lower belvedere is off the Rennweg. There you will find a museum of baroque art.

The **Schonbrunn Palace** is on the west side of the city, and is one of Vienna's most famous sights. The name means 'beautiful fountains' after those that were built over the natural springs in the 17th century, when the Emperor Matthias had his hunting lodge on the site. The lodge was burnt down by the Turks in 1863, and Leopold I decided to build a new summer residence for his family. The Gloriette (triumphal arches) was completed in 1775, and was used in those days for innumerable social events.

The palace was the favourite residence of Maria Theresia, whose daughter Marie Antoinette, of French Revolution fame, spent her childhood here. Mozart performed here for the Empress at the age of six. Napoleon had his headquarters here in the early 1800s, and his son, whose mother was Archduchess Marie-Louise, was raised here by his grandfather Emperor Franz. Emperor Franz Josef was born here and died here, after 68 years on the throne, and it was at Schonbrunn that Emperor Karl I abdicated, bringing an end to 636 years of Hapsburg rule.

Today forty-two rooms of the palace are open to the public and are not to be missed. Allow plenty of time for a visit as there is so much to take in, and time is needed to wander through the gardens, and visit the Gloriette for a magnificent view of the city.

Salzburg

The beautiful city of Salzburg is the capital of the province of the same name, and has a population of 145,000. The picturesque Salzach River flows through the centre of the city, which is famous as the birthplace of the composer Wolfgang Amadeus Mozart. It also was the location for the movie classic *The Sound of Music* as the Trapp family were residents of Salzburg.

The old town is on the left side of the Salzach, dominated by the Fortress Hohensalzburg; the new town on the right of the river nestles beneath the Kapuzinerberg (the Capuchin monastery/fortress).

History

Historians agree that parts of Salzburg were inhabited as far back as 3000 BC. At various times during its history the town was home to Illyrians, Celts, and then Romans, who called it Juvavum. The town became an important trade centre, and was raised by the Romans to the status of a municipium, but during the migration of Germanic tribes, the settlement was destroyed.

It was the 7th century that saw the beginnings of today's city, when Bishop Rupertus founded the Benedictine monastery of St Peter, which became the seat of the bishops, later archbishops, for many centuries. The first cathedral was erected by Bishop Virgil in the 8th century, and work on the present cathedral began in 1614 under Archbishop Markus Sitticus.

This religious importance has resulted in a wealth of ecclesiastic architecture, as well as palaces, museums and many interesting period houses.

Tourist Information

The information office is in Mozartplatz, and has all the information, maps, brochures, etc, that are available.

Local Transport

The city has a good public transport system, but for the visitor walking tours are the way to go. If you run out of energy in the old city, continue your tour in a fiaker (horse-drawn cab). Their starting point is in the Residenzplatz.

Accommodation

Ramada, is a superior first class hotel in the midtown area. Facilities include restaurant, bar, health club, swimming pool, shops and beauty salon.

Dorint Hotel, is a first class hotel in the midtown area. Facilities include restaurant and bar.

There are several youth hostels in Salzburg:

Salzburg Nonntal, Josef-Preis Allee 18, ph (662) 842 6700.

Eduard-Heinrich Haus, Eduard Heinrich Strasse 2, ph (662) 25 976, fax (662) 27 980.

Glockengasse, Glockengasse 8, ph (662) 876 241.

Walserfeld, Schulstrasse 18, ph (662) 851 377, fax (662) 853 301.

Food & Drink

Coffee houses and restaurants abound in Salzburg, especially along the banks of the Salzach. The city even has its own special dish - Salzburger Nockerin which translates roughly as 'souffle style of Salzburg'. It is lemon-flavoured and delicious.

Sightseeing

A walking tour of the old city begins at the information office in Mozartplatz.

The platz has a large statue of Mozart, but apparently his sons were not too impressed with the likeness when it was unveiled in 1842. The tour then winds its way to the **Alter Markt** (old market), a photogenic square formed by old houses that is home to: **St Florian's Fountain**; the **Smallest House of Salzburg,** now owned by an optician; **Cafe Tomaselli** (1703) the oldest coffee house in the city; and possibly a few stalls reminiscent of the square's original function.

The tour then enters the pedestrian Getreidegasse and passes the **old town hall** (1407), then a suitably chastened McDonald's sign, and **burghers' houses** from the 15th to 18th centuries. Many little lanes and alleys run of the street near this section, and they contain interesting shops and coffee houses. Also note in this street and many others in the old city, the hanging shingles outside the buildings. These are mostly descriptive of the profession or trade of the owner, and were designed before people could read and write. Some of them are quite amusing.

The most visited house on Getreidegasse is no. 9, **Mozart Geburtshaus**, where Mozart was born on January 27, 1756, and lived until 1763. The house now contains a museum of Mozart memorabilia, including his childhood violin, many other instruments that he played, letters, manuscripts, etc - very interesting. Salzburg is very proud of Mozart and has several yearly events that celebrate his music - Mozart Week in late January, festivals at Easter and through all of August, and the famous Salzburger Kulturtage in October.

Continuing to the right at the end of Getreidegasse brings you to **Anton-Neumayr Platz**, where there is a statue of the Virgin Mary dating from 1691. On the left is the **Monchsberg lift**, which ascends inside the rock to a terrace that offers a fantastic view over the city. It is also the entrance to the Cafe Winkler and its gambling casino.

Next on the tour is Museumplatz, where there are a couple of museums, then around the corner is **St Mark's church** (1699). Follow the map for a few twists and turns then stop at the traffic lights on Sigmundsplatz to admire the **Horse-Pond**. The paintings on the rear wall were restored in 1916, but the main attraction is the *Horse Tamer* which was sculpted by Michael Bernhard Mandl in 1695.

The walk then visits Universitatsplatz where there is a food market every day except Sunday, and the **Church of the Immaculata** (1707), which has to be one of the most beautiful Baroque churches. Follow directions to the Hofstallgasse and there is the **Festspielhaus** (playhouse), which is actually two playhouses, the new containing a 2000+ auditorium, and the old seating 1300 people. Nearby is the open galleried theatre that was the venue for tournaments and animal-baiting in the olden days. Continue on into Franciskanergasse to the **Franciscan Church**, consecrated in 1223, and well worth a look-see. Exit by the south door and walk under an arch into the courtyard of **St**

Salzburg: Gardens of Mirabell Palace

Peter's Abbey, founded in 690 by St Rupert. Be prepared now to be overwhelmed and educated as you wander from church to tomb to chapel, to cemetery to mausoleum, ending at **St Margaret's Chapel** with its beautifully cared-for graves.

Next stop is the **Hohensalzburg fortress** (1077) which can be reached by taking the funicular from its lower station in Festungsgasse. There are great panoramic views of the city from the fortress, but there are also interesting guided tours available that include the state apartments, the cells and torture chamber, and the fortress and Rainer museums.

The **Cathedral** (Dom) is in Domplatz and can seat 10,000 people. There have been several cathedrals on this site, and the present church was consecrated in 1628. The dome was completely destroyed and the interior badly damaged during World War II, so it was restored and reconsecrated in 1959. Its bells are the largest in Europe. The cathedral has much for those interested in art and sculpture, and there is a museum that was inaugurated on the 1200th anniversary of the cathedral that has an unusual collection of religious memorabilia. Heading now towards the **Residenzplatz**, watch out for the **Excavations Museum** which has artifacts found on the cathedral site that range from early Roman times to the Middle Ages.

Residenzplatz is the largest of Salzburg's squares and it contains the largest baroque fountain in the world. It is also home to *the Residence*, completed in 1619 and the seat of the archbishops until 1803. Conducted tours are offered and it is the best way to view the place. The building contains some wonderful works of art.

On the other side of the square is the **New Residence**, erected in 1602. It has the **Glockenspiel Tower** which plays works by Mozart every day at 7am, 11am and 6pm.

The only place left on this walking tour is **St Michael's Church** on the north side of Residenzplatz. It dates from the year 800 and is the oldest parish church in the city.

It might be a good idea to take time out now to enjoy a stroll along the river before crossing one of the bridges over the Salzach to the new town.

First stop is the **Mirabell gardens**, which are very formally laid out and include a large fountain with sculptures that are supposed to represent the four elements. At one end of the gardens stands what's left of the **Schloss Mirabell**, which was mostly destroyed by fire in 1818.

In the Makartplatz is the **Landestheater**; next door is the **Salzburg Marionette Theatre**; adjacent is the **Mozarteum**, an international music academy; outshining them all is the **Church of the Holy Trinity**; and just off the square in Theatergasse is the Cafe Bazar, which is a popular artists' haunt. There are two more churches in this area - **St Sebastian's** in the Linzergasse, and the **Loreto Church** in Paris-Lodron Strasse.

Finally, there is the **Capuchin Monastery**, and a magnificent panoramic view is available from the bastion below the monastery.

Belgium

Belgium is a democracy under a limited monarchy. It is a very densely populated country, with more than 10 million people living in its 30,497 sq km. Belgium still has the boundaries won by the revolution of 1930, in spite of the cultural differences between the Walloons and the Flemish citizens.

Language, though, is the chief distinction between the two groups - the Walloons speak French, and the Flemish speak Dutch. Both languages are regarded as official and equal, and people who deal with the general public are required to speak both. People in the hospitality industry usually speak English as well, so assistance will not be far away should you need it.

Today Belgium, together with Holland and Luxembourg, is a part of the Benelux, or Low Countries, with practically no border control between the members. The headquarters of the EEC (European Economic Community) is located in Belgium's capital, Brussels.

Climate

There are seasonal extremes, although the climate is mainly temperate. The hottest month is July and the coldest is January.

Entry Regulations

A valid passport of at least six months is required by all visitors. Visas are not required for periods of less than three months, and no vaccinations are required for any international traveller.

The duty free allowance is 200 cigarettes, 100 cigarillos, 50 cigars or 250 grams tobacco, 1 litre of spirits or sparkling wine, and 2 litres of non-sparkling wine.

There is no restriction on the import or export of local or foreign currencies.

Currency

The currency of the land is the Belgian Franc (BFr), which is divided into 100 centimes, but the smallest coin in circulation is 50 centimes. Approximate rates of exchange, which should be used as a guide only, are:

A$	= 21BFr
Can$	= 22BFr
NZ$	= 24BFr
S$	= 22BFr
UK£	= 46BFr
US$	= 28BFr

Belgian francs are accepted in Luxembourg, but there is no reciprocal arrangement.

Banks are generally open 9am-4pm Mon-Fri, and post offices are open 9am-5pm Mon-Fri.

Shops are normally open 9am-6pm Mon-Sat. Credit cards are widely accepted in the major cities, but not in the smaller towns.

Telephone

International direct dialling is available and the International code is 00, the country code is 32. The area code for Brussels is 02. Emergency numbers are - Police 101; Ambulance and Fire Brigade 100.

Driving

Motorways connect most cities and towns in the country, and there are no toll charges. Driving is on the right and the speed limits are:

Built-up areas	- 60kph
Outside built-up areas	- 90kph
Motorways	- 120kph.

The Royal Automobile Club of Belgium (RACB) is at rue d'Arlon 53 - 1040 Brussels, ph 287 0980.

Miscellaneous

Local time is GMT + 1 (Central European Time) with daylight saving in force, late March to late September.

Electricity is 220v AC, with round two pin plugs. In old houses it may be 120v but they are changing to 220v.

Health - Belgium has good health services, but they can be expensive. Health insurance is highly recommended.

Brussels

Brussels is a small Walloonic-Flemish city that has become an administrative centre of Europe with excellent railway connections and Common Market Offices. It is a charming city of contrasts, and offers much to the traveller.

History

Belgium was a prosperous part of the Frankish Kingdom under Charlemagne, and Flemish cloth was much sought after abroad. After his death the country was partitioned, leading to the rise of powerful local lords, such as the Counts of Flanders.

Nevertheless the country flourished, until it became involved in European affairs. Belgians became subject to the Kingdom of France, then to the Dukes of Burgundy, then to the Spanish and Austrian Hapsburgs.

In the 16th century, Brussels was the political capital of the emperor Charles V, who had been born in Belgium.

The Revolt of the Netherlands, although successful in the north was defeated in Belgium, and Hapsburg rule was reinstated. The country became the scene of the warring Bourbons and Hapsburgs. A time of French rule followed, then a brief reunion with Holland, before the revolution of 1830 gained independence.

Tourist Information

The Brussels Information Centrum (TIB), Grand Place 1, 1000 Brussels, ph 513 8940.

General Commissioner of Tourism, rue du Marche aux Herbes 61, 1000 Brussels, ph 504 0400.

Local Transport

Brussels has a metro (underground) system, buses and trams. For information on schedules or prices, ph 515 3064.

The metro stations have works of art for sale, and a catalogue can be obtained from the information offices.

Accommodation

Renaissance Hotel is a deluxe hotel in the downtown area. Facilities include restaurant, bar, coffee shop, health club, swimming pool and shops.

Hilton is a superior first class hotel in the downtown area. Facilities include restaurant, bar, coffee shop, shops and beauty salon.

Sheraton is a superior first class hotel in the downtown area. Facilities include restaurant, bar, coffee shop, disco, health club, swimming pool and shops.

There are three youth hostels in Brussels:

Jean Nihon, 4 rue de le'Elephant, ph (2) 410 3858, fax (2) 410 3905.

Jacques Brel, rue de la Sablonniere 30, ph (2) 218 0187, fax (2) 217 2005.

Heilig, Geeststraat 2, ph (2) 511 0436, fax (2) 512 0711

Food and Drink

The main meal is eaten in the middle of the day, and consists of very generous portions. Afternoon coffee, usually with a pastry of some kind, is around 4pm, with supper at 7pm.

The national drinks are coffee and beer, and there are over 350 brands of beer available. This is not counting the local ales available in some of the villages. There are no licensing hours, but the sale of spirits in cafes and restaurants is forbidden.**The obvious national food item would have to be Brussels Sprouts.**

Sightseeing

The **Grand Place**, the centre of social, economic and political activities from the 12th century, was almost entirely destroyed in 48 hours in August 1695, by order of Louis XIV. However it was rebuilt in less than four years in a blend of Italian and Flemish

Town Hall, Brussels

Baroque style. From June to September, from 9pm, there is a sound and light show. The most prominent building on the Place is the **Town Hall** (Hotel de Ville), which is open to visitors Mon-Fri 9am-4.30pm. The other buildings are houses of the various Guilds (associations of craftpersons), eg the King House (Maison du Roi) which now houses a Communal Museum, was the Bread House in the 13th century.

To the left past the Town Hall, a short walk leads to the corner of rue de l'Etuve & rue du Chene, and the well-known but slightly vulgar **Manneken-Pis Fountain**. The small bronze statuette, which dates back to 1619, is called 'the oldest citizen of the city' and represents a young hero from Brussels' folklore. The figure owns a varied and abundant wardrobe that is housed in the Communal Museum in the Grand Place.

Another small part of the old town is found on the way to the cathedral, around Petite rue de Bouchers, with its elegant restaurants and St Hubert Galleries. The beautiful, gothic **St Michael's Cathedral** dates from the Middle Ages, and contains the graves of the Dukes of Brabant, the Archdukes Albert and Isabelle, and Charles of Lorraine.

The **Saint-Hubert Royal Galleries** were built in 1846, and were the first covered shopping arcades in Europe. (Many people thought that Bern had the first.) They are made of up three distinct parts - the King's Gallery, the Queen's Gallery and the Princes' Gallery.

The other main shopping area is around rue Neuve.
The Palace of the Nation, in Parc de Bruxelles, on rue de la Loi was built in 1783 for the sovereign Council of Brabant. Called the Palace of the States General in 1817, it became the Palace of the Nation after 1830 and is where both houses of Parliament sit. The **Parc de Bruxelles** was formerly the hunting ground of the Dukes of Brabant, and was converted to a French garden in the 18th century. In 1830 it was the main battlefield in the war between Dutch troops and the Belgian insurgents.

La Place des Palais (Palaces' Square) is bordered by the **Palais des Academies**, the **Royal Palace**, and the **Palais des Beaux-Arts**. The first was the former residence of the Prince of Orange, and was built between 1823 and 1826. It has housed the Belgian Royal Academy since 1876. The Royal Palace is the most important of the trio, and it

BRUSSELS

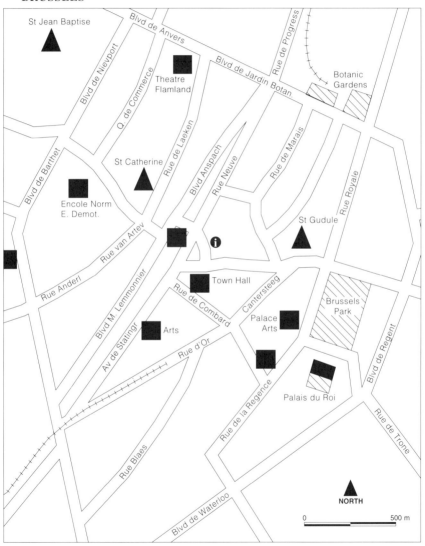

owes its Louis XVI appearance to King Leopold II, who had alterations to the facade carried out in 1904. It is the official residence of the present king, Albert II. The Palace of Fine Arts is west of the square and is a spacious building, mostly underground. It has many exhibition rooms, a movie theatre and a concert hall. It was built in 1930.

The nearby **Place Royale** was built in the 18th century during the reign of Charles of Lorraine. The equestrian statue in the centre is of Godefroid de Bouillon, and behind it is the St Jacques-sur-Coudenberg Church.

The **Congress Column**, off Konings Sraat, rises to a height of 47m and is topped by a statue of Leopold I, the first king of the Belgians. There is access to a lookout that provides a panoramic view of the city. At the foot of the column are two unknown soldiers from the World Wars.

Rue de la Loi runs south-east from the city centre to the **Parc du Cinquantenaire** which is home to the **Cinquantenaire**, a monumental arched structure inspired by Leopold II and completed in 1905. The **Army Museum** and the **Royal Museum of Art and History** are housed either side of the arch.

Denmark

Denmark is a constitutional monarchy, with a total area of 43,069 sq km, made up of 407 islands and a large peninsula, Jutland, bordered by northern Germany. The population is 5.2 million, one-quarter of whom live in the capital Copenhagen.

Considered by many to be the prettiest of the Scandinavian countries, Denmark is also the most prosperous, which is evidenced by the many manor houses of various architectural styles and periods.

Denmark has been settled since prehistoric times, and there are many passage graves, particularly in the south, that are open for inspection.

The language of the country is Danish, but English is widely understood and spoken.

Climate
Denmark is situated in a temperate zone, and the weather is often wet and windy. Winter brings snow and rain.

Average temperatures in Copenhagen are: January max 3C, min -1C; June max 21C, min 13C.

Entry Regulations
Visitors must have a valid passport, but visas are not required. It is always a good idea, though, to check with an embassy or consulate in your own country before departure.

The duty free allowance is 200 cigarettes or 50 cigars or 250g tobacco, 50g perfume or 250ml eau de toilette, 0.5kg coffee; 100g tea; and other goods to a maximum value of Dkr350.

No vaccinations are required.

Currency

The currency of the land is the Krone (plural Kroner), and 1Dkr = 100 ore. Approximate rates of exchange, which should be used as a guide only, are:

A$	= Dkr4.63
Can$	= Dkr4.30
NZ$	= Dkr4.00
S$	= Dkr4.20
UK£	= Dkr8.90
US$	= Dkr5.85.

Notes are in denominations of Dkr1000, 500, 100 and 50, and coins are Dkr20, 10, 5, 2 and 1, 50 and 20 ore (ore amounts are rounded off when paying cash but remain on cheques).

Banks are open Mon-Fri 9.30am-4pm, Thurs until 6pm, and some currency exchange offices are open until 10pm. Keep in mind that the banks may refuse to exchange large foreign bank notes.*Visa* and *MasterCard* are widely accepted, but not so *American Express* except in major hotels and shops.

Post offices are open Mon-Fri 9am/10am-5pm/5.30pm, Sat 9am-noon.

Generally shops are open Mon-Wed 9am-5.30pm, Thurs 9am-7pm, Fri 9am-8pm, Sat 9am-noon, but some do not open until 10am and then stay open longer. In the country areas most shops close for lunch (noon-2pm). Shops in the tourist areas, and all bakeries and kiosks are open on Sunday.

Telephone

International direct dialling is available and the International code is 009, the Country code 45.

Driving

Traffic drives on the right-hand side of the road, and passes on the left. Headlights have to be on 24 hours a day.

Speed limits are:

Expressways	110km/h
Dual carriageways	80km/h
Single carriageways	80km/h
Town areas	50km/h.

When driving in the countryside it is best to avoid the

smaller side-roads which are mostly used by cyclists, many travelling in family groups.

The maximum blood alcohol limit is .05.

Miscellaneous

Standard time is GMT + 1.

Electricity is 220 volts AC. It is advisable to carry an adaptor for your appliances.

Health - It is advisable to have private medical insurance, especially if you are travelling from a country that is outside the European Union.

Tipping - As a service fee is included in hotel and restaurant bills, it is not necessary to tip unless you feel that you have been given very good service.

Copenhagen

Copenhagen is situated on the island of Sjaelland, in the north-eastern part of Denmark, across the Sound from Sweden's industrial city of Malmö. It is the country's capital and main city.

It is the residence of the monarch, the seat of government, parliament and the supreme court. The city is also the centre of trade and industry in the country.

It is also a colourful city with a rather relaxed ambience.

History

The inner town of Copenhagen has been inhabited for at least 6000 years. A thousand years ago it was a small fishing village called *Havn* (harbour), but it was important because of its great natural harbour and its position on the main trade route. In 1167 Bishop Absalon, Bishop of Roskilde, built a castle on a small island and fortified the town. Soon it became known as *Kiobmaennehavn* (the merchants' harbour), which lead to *Kobenhavn* its present name in Danish.

In the 15th century the city passed to the Crown of Denmark, and a university and a naval base were established. Copenhagen prospered and was the principal city of a realm that included Norway, Iceland, southern Sweden, Schleswig-Holstein, as well as Denmark.

The city's importance made it a target and, in the civil and religious strife of the Protestant Reformation, it was often sacked. In the 17th century it prospered under the energetic builder King Christian IV and foreign trade grew enormously. Buildings from this period include the Borsen, the Holmens Church and the Palace of Rosenborg. The 17th century brought a devastating war with Sweden, and for two years Copenhagen was besieged by the Swedish King Charles X Gustavus - unsuccessfully.

Great tracts of the city were destroyed by fire in 1827 and 1795, but these were only temporary setbacks in a period of rapid growth that came to an end with the Napoleonic Wars.

In 1801, the British fleet attacked Copenhagen without a declaration of war, to keep the Danes from closing the Baltic Sea. That ferocious battle, one of Horatio Nelson's great triumphs, ended in a truce, but the British bombarded the city again in 1807 and left much of it in ruins.

It took some time for Copenhagen to recover, but the 19th century brought increasing wealth. In a break with the past, the city's walls were pulled down in 1856, and expansion began into the surrounding districts. In the 1870s industrialisation began in earnest, and a free port was set up in 1894.

During World War II, Copenhagen was occupied by German forces, but the city suffered little damage. The widespread popular resistance to the occupation forces is commemorated in the Museum of the Danish Resistance Movement. In recent years, Copenhagen has become one of the leading cultural and artistic centres of northern Europe.

Tourist Information

There is a tourist information office at 1 Bernstorffsgade (near the Tivoli Gardens), ph 33 11 13 25; and another at Norregade 7A, 1165 Copenhagen K, ph 33 13 70 07.

Copenhagen 'This Week' is a free monthly magazine that lists everything a visitor needs to know about the city.

Local Transport

Copenhagen has efficient bus and subway systems. The subway is called S-tog, ph 33 14 17 01, and accepts Eurail passes. Bus fares are paid as you board, and the driver will have change. City maps have bus and subway routes marked, but when in doubt ask one of the locals. They are always happy to help. If you wish to enquire about bus timetables, ph 36 45 45 45.

There are plenty of taxis in the city, and they can be flagged down anywhere. If you are travelling in a group of, say, four people, it will often be cheaper to hire a taxi than take a bus.

Accommodation

Hotel Palace, Raadhuspladsen 57 - restaurant, cocktail bar - Dkr1320.

Hotel Alexandra, HC Andersens Boulevard 8 (on Town Hall Square - restaurant, cocktail bar - Dkr1065.

Komfort Hotel, Loengangstraede 27 (near the Town Hall) - restaurant, cocktail bar - Dkr972.

Food and Drink

Restaurants include a 25% tax plus a 15% tip, so eating out is an expensive experience. Danish specialties are pastries (*wienerbrod*), open sandwiches (*smorrebrod*), and hot dogs (*polse*), but don't expect those in their native land to look exactly the same as the ones you love back home.

If you want to sample all the traditional Danish dishes in the same meal, visit the *Bistro Restaurant* in the Central Station, ph 33 14 12 32, and enjoy a *koldt bord*. This is the local version of the Swedish smorgasbord.

Shopping

The main department stores are *Illum*, ph 33 14 40 02, and *Magasin*, ph 33 11 44 33, and both are on Stroget (pronounced stroyet), the pedestrian shopping mall.

Scala is a complex of boutiques, restaurants and entertainment venues, and is worth a visit. It is on Vesterbrogade, across from the Tivoli.

Shops are open Mon-Fri 9.30am-7pm, Sat 9am-2pm.

Sightseeing

A walking tour of Copenhagen begins at **Radhuspladsen** (Town Hall Square), which was once the west end of town. Built in the Italian Renaissance style, there is a statue of the city's founder above the hall's portal. The Town Hall is open to the public Mon-Fri 10am-3pm, and admission is free. The walk up the 300 steps to the tower and the best view of the city, however, will set you back 10Dkr, ph 33 66 25 82.

Look up the walls of the building on the square that is opposite the Stroget, and you will see the city's 'weather girls' - riding a bike if it is going to be fine, armed with an umbrella if it is not.

Nearby are the **Tivoli Gardens**, which were built in 1843 outside the city walls. The first public amusement park in Europe, the Tivoli was built to appease the people's discontent with their lot, and it succeeded. Covering 20 acres, the gardens offer rides, games, marching bands, roulette wheels, funny mirrors, restaurants and many happy hours. Admission is 38Dkr, and there are many free concerts, puppet shows, etc, but if you want to participate in all the rides, you should think seriously of purchasing an all-day pass for 160Dkr. The park is open daily 10am-midnight (late April to mid-September), closed off-season, ph 33 15 10 01.

It should be kept in mind that this amusement park is over 150 years old, and was around a long time before Walt Disney began opening up his 'lands' and 'worlds'.

The **train station**, behind the Tivoli, was obviously also built outside the city walls.

To the right of the Town Hall is a statue of Copenhagen's favourite son, **Hans Christian Andersen**, and to the left of the Hall is the **Lur-Blowers sculpture**. Original lurs, which were popular instruments three and half thousand years ago, are on display in the National Museum.

The **Ny Carlsberg Glyptotek**, cnr Hans Christian Andersens Boulevard and Tietgengade, has the largest collection of antique art in Northern Europe, along with many 19th century French and Danish sculptures and paintings, that include works by the Impressionists. Open Tues-Sun 10am-4pm (winter noon-3pm) and admission is 15Dkr, ph 33 41 91 41.

The **National Museum** is at Vestergade 10, and has a very good collection of Danish history from the earliest times presented in chronological order with English explanations. The museum is open Tues-Sun 10am-5pm and admission is 30Dkr, ph 33 13 44 11.

The northern boundary of the museum is the Frederiksholms Canal, which you cross via the Marble Bridge, which was built in 1775. This leads to **Slotsholmen** (castle island), which has much to offer the visitor. Firstly there is the **Christiansborg Palace**, the fifth to be built on this site, which has housed since 1928, the Parliament, the Supreme Court, the Foreign Office and the Royal Chambers. Guided tours of 22 of the Queen's reception rooms are available Tues-Sun at 11am, 1pm and 3pm (May-September); Tues, Thurs and Sun 11am, 3pm (Oct-April), and cost 27Dkr, ph 33 92 64 92. There are tours of the parliament.

In the basement of the palace tower are the foundations of the **original castle** built by Bishop Absalon. The exhibit is open daily 9.30am-3.30pm (closed Mon and Sat in the off-season) and entry is 15Dkr.

Other parts of the palace that can be visited include the **Royal Mews** with its coach museum, a **Theatre Museum**, and the **Palace Chapel**. Next door to that is a museum housing the works of **Bertel Thorvaldsen**, 1770-1844, and in fact it also houses the great neoclassical sculptor himself. The museum also offers one of the best views of the city, across the **Gammel Strand**, the departure point for harbour cruises.

Still on Slotsholmen are: **Christiansborg Slotsplads**, with its equestrian statue of Frederick VII; the **Royal Library**, built in 1906; the **Royal Brewery**, commissioned by Christian IV; as was the **Arsenal**; and the Renaissance **Exchange**, with its dragon tail spire. Still there is more to see.

From the Palace Chapel, walk along Kobmagergade to the **Stroget** and the **Amagertorv**, the square in the centre of the city. House no 6 on the square is the main exhibition and sales rooms of **Royal Porcelain**.

The next attraction you can take or leave, depending on your point of view. At Kobmagergade 24 is the **Museum of Erotica**, which has as its theme the role Denmark played in the 1970s in the legalisation of pornography. There are other exhibits on sexual practices down through the ages, and similar items of bad taste, and the admission price is 45Dkr.

The next stop is also not compulsory, unless you are travelling with children. The **Toy Museum** is at Valken-dorfsgade 13.

Following the Stroget to its end at **Kongens Nytorv** (King's New Square), which dates from the 17th century. Buildings here include the **Royal Theatre** and **Charlottenborg**, which houses the Royal Academy of Fine Arts. The pretty centre of the square is called the **Krinsen**, and the man on the horse is Charles V.

Now we come to a very colourful part of the city, a harbour extension called **Nyhavn**. Apart from the old sailing ships, there are plenty of pubs and people that combine to make a visit worth while. Hans Christian Andersen was enamoured of this area and lived for a time in three different houses - Nyhavn 18, 20 and 67.

At the end of the canal, turn right and walk fast the ferry docks to the **Harbour Promenade**. Continue past the 6m bronze copy of Michelangelo's *David* to the **Amalienhave Park**, which is between the harbour and the **Amalienborg Palace**, the home of the Danish royal family. There are actually four identical rococo palaces: Queen Margrethe II and family live in the one to the left of the harbour side entrance of the square. Prince Frederik, the heir apparent to the throne lives directly opposite.

There is a changing of the guard at noon when the queen is in residence, but frankly, it is not worth organising everything to be there then.

The **Christian VIII Palace** is open to the public and has exhibits from the time of Christian IX (1863-1906).

The statue in the centre of square is Frederick V, and locals like to think that he is riding towards the Marmorkirken, which took 150 years to build.

Continuing north onto the Bredgade, the next stop is the **Museum of Decorative and Applied Arts**, which has the best collection of Japanese arts and crafts outside of Japan.

At the end of the Bredgade, turn right into the Esplanaden, and you will be able to see the **Freedom Museum** (Frihedsmuseet), which details the Danish Resistance against the Germans during World War II. It is open daily 10am-4pm (May to mid-September), Tues-Sun 11am-3pm (rest of the year), ph 33 13 77 14.

There are two attractions remaining on our walking tour. The first is the **Gefion Fountain**, and the last is the **Little Mermaid**, the symbol of Copenhagen. The statue is, of course, based on a character from a Hans Christian Andersen fairy tale. The sculptor was Edvard Eiksen, whose wife posed for him, and the work was finished in 1913. I would rate this statue as one of life's disappointments. Whoever heard of a mermaid with two legs that ended in flippers? We all know that they have a fishtail.

After all this walking, it might be a good idea to return to the city by taxi, or by bus 1, 6 or 9 from Kastellet Park near the Freedom Museum.

There are a few other interesting places to visit in Copenhagen, but they do not comfortably fit into a walking tour.

To the west of the main station is the **Carlsberg Brewery**, and there are free tours and tasting sessions available Mon-Fri 11am and 2pm, ph 33 27 13 14 ext 1312. To get there take bus 6 to 140 Ny Carlsberg Vej.

Also this way is the **Royal Copenhagen Porcelain Manufactory**, Vestergade 10, also has tours on weekdays and 'seconds' available to keen-eyed purchasers.

Last, but not least, is the **Rosenborg Palace**, which can be reached by taking the subway to Norreport Station, then walking in a northerly direction. The palace was built between 1606 and 1617, and visitors can see apartments relating to the various kings from Christian IV (1588) to Frederick IV (1863). Also on display are the **Danish crown jewels**. Guides are available, and the palace is open daily 10am-4pm (June-August); 11am-3pm May, September and October; and Tues- Fri and Sun 11am-2pm in the off-season. It is best to visit Rosenborg in the middle of the day, however, as there is no interior electricity, ph 33 15 32 86.

FRANCE

1. Ain
2. Aisne
3. Allier
4. Alpes-de-Haute-Provence
5. Alpes-Maritimes
6. Ardèche
7. Ardennes
8. Ariège
9. Aube
10. Aude
11. Aveyron
12. Bas-Rhin
13. Belfort
14. Bouches-du-Rhône
15. Calvados
16. Cantal
17. Charente
18. Charente-Maritime
19. Cher
20. Corrèze
21. Corse du Sud
22. Côte-d'Or
23. Côtes-du-Nord
24. Creuse
25. Deux-Sèvres
26. Dordogne
27. Doubs
28. Drôme
29. Essonne
30. Eure
31. Eure-et-Loir
32. Finistère
33. Gard
34. Gers
35. Gironde
36. Haute-Corse
37. Haute-Garonne
38. Haute-Loire
39. Haute-Marne
40. Hautes-Alpes
41. Haute-Saône
42. Haute-Savoie
43. Hautes-Pyrénées
44. Haute-Vienne
45. Haut-Rhin
46. Hauts-de-Seine
47. Hérault
48. Ille-et-Vilaine
49. Indre
50. Indre-et-Loire
51. Isère
52. Jura
53. Landes
54. Loire
55. Loire-Atlantique
56. Loiret
57. Loir-et-Cher
58. Lot
59. Lot-et-Garonne
60. Lozère
61. Maine-et-Loire

62. Manche
63. Marne
64. Mayenne
65. Meurthe-et-Moselle
66. Meuse
67. Morbihan
68. Moselle
69. Nièvre
70. Nord
71. Oise
72. Orne
73. Pas-de-Calais
74. Puy-de-Dôme
75. Pyrénées-Atlantiques
76. Pyrénées-Orientales
77. Rhône
78. Saône-et-Loire

79. Sarthe
80. Savoie
81. Seine-et-Marne
82. Seine-Maritime
83. Seine-Saint-Denis
84. Somme
85. Tarn
86. Tarn-et-Garonne
87. Val-de-Marne
88. Val-d'Oise
89. Var
90. Vaucluse
91. Vendée
92. Vienne
93. Vosges
94. Yonne
95. Yvelines

France

France is the second largest country in Europe, with an area of 547,026 sq km, and a population of about 55 million. The French Fifth Republic has a constitution that was adopted in 1958 and amended in 1962. There is a strong President, elected for a 7-year term, a Prime Minister appointed by the President, and a parliament of two houses.

The capital is Paris where approximately 4 million people live. The language of the country is, of course, French, but English is spoken in big stores, banks, hotels and tourist offices.

Climate

There are wide variations in the climate, depending on the region. Inland has hot summers, and there is usually heavy winter snow in the Alps.

The averages for *Paris* are 13-24C in July, and 0-6 in January.

Marseille on the Mediterranean coast averages 18-28C in August, 3-12C in January.

Entry Regulations

Visitors must have a current passport, and people from member countries of the EC, Canada, the United States and New Zealand, amongst others, do not require visas. Australians and Singaporeans, however, do require visas.

The duty free allowance is 400 cigarettes or 100 cigars or 500 gm of tobacco, 1 litre of spirits (more than 22% alcoholic strength) or up to 2 litres of spirits (maximum of 22% alcoholic strength). Bit more than other countries allow.

There is no restriction on the import of local currency, however it is only permissible to convert French Francs into foreign currencies up to the equivalent of F5,000.

No vaccinations are required for any international traveller.

Currency

The currency of the land is the French Franc, abbreviated to F or FRF, which is divided into 100 centimes. Approximate exchange rates, which should be used as a guide only, are:

A$	= 3.65FRF
Can$	= 3.50FRF
NZ$	= 3.20FRF
S$	= 3.50FRF
UK£	= 7.95FRF
US$	= 5.00FRF

Notes are in denominations of 500, 200, 100, 50 and 20 Francs, and coins are 10, 5, 2 and 1 Francs and 50, 20, 10 and 5 centimes.

Banks are usually open 9am-noon and 2-4pm weekdays, but closed either Sat or Mon. They also close early on the day before a public holiday.

Post offices in the main cities are usually open Mon-Fri 8.30am-7pm, and Sat 8.30am-12.30pm.

Shops in Paris are usually open Mon-Sat 10am-7pm, but outside of Paris they tend to close for a couple of hours around lunch time, and may be closed on Mon afternoon.

Credit cards are widely accepted in the major cities.

Telephone

International direct dialling is available and the International code is 19, the country code 33. The telephone system has only two regions - Paris and the rest of France. The area code for Paris is (1), the rest of France does not have an area code.

Note:

For calls from Paris to any of the provinces, it is necessary to dial 16, then the local 8-figure numbers; for calls from any of the provinces to Paris, dial 16 (1) then the local 8-figure number. But, if dialling Paris from, say Sydney, you would dial 0011 + 33 + 1 + the local 8-figure number. In other words, the 16 is not used for overseas calls.

Emergency numbers are: Police 17; Fire 18; Operator 13.

Driving

To hire a car it is necessary to have a valid driving licence, held for at least one year, and a passport. It is compulsory to wear a seat-belt, and children under 10 years old may not travel in the front. Speed limits change with the weather, and are as follows:

Road System	Km/hour	
	Dry	Wet
Expressways	130	110
Dual Carriageways	110	100
Single Carriageways	90	80
Town Area	45-60	35-50

Miscellaneous

Local time is GMT + 1 (Central European Time). In the summer it changes to daylight saving. Daylight saving operates from late March to late September.

Electricity - 220v AC, with round-pin plugs.

Health - France has no specific health warnings, but adequate medical insurance is recommended.

Paris

If there were to be a capital of Europe, it would have to be Paris. Whereas London caters for young people, Paris is for everyone.

Even though the twenty inner suburbs (arrondissements) are influenced by customs from other lands, Paris remains very French.

History

Before the time of Christ there was a small town in the middle of a river, and it was called Lutetia. Here lived a tribe called the Parisii. The Romans, led by Julius Caesar, conquered the Parisii, extended the town onto the left bank of the river and fortified it. This town became Paris.

In 496, Clovis, the Christian leader of the Franks, defeated the German tribes and established a new hereditary dynasty, the Merovingian. He selected Paris as the capital, and succeeding rulers added to and beautified the city.

In 886, Norman invaders sacked Paris and it was reduced to a small island town once more. This is now the Ile de la Cite. The Normans were given Normandy as a consolation prize, and things returned to normal.

Kings came and went, and at one stage were almost abandoned in favour of feudal lords, and then came Hugh Capet, who was crowned King of all France in 987. There followed 400 years of stability, with Paris becoming established as the political, economic and cultural capital of the country. The Sorbonne, the Louvre and Notre Dame were built during the reign of Philip Augustus (1180-1223).

The Golden Age of the French monarchy was during the reigns of Louis XIII, Louis XIV (the Sun King, who built Versailles) and Louis XV. Then came Louis XVI and his Queen Marie Antoinette, and in 1789, the Revolution, and then Napoleon.

Following Napoleon there was a restoration of the monarchy, then the 2nd Republic lasted from 1848 until 1852. This was followed by the 2nd Empire, then the 3rd Republic, then the Vichy Government during the second world war.

When Paris was liberated in 1944, General Charles de Gaulle's government was recognised by the Allies, and a new constitution was drawn up in 1946. There followed a period of instability, then a new constitution saw the beginning of the 5th Republic, which is the present government.

Tourist Information

The Office de Tourisme de Paris, 127, ave des Champs- Elysees, ph 49 52 53 54, is open daily 9am-8pm (closed May 1, Dec 25 & Jan 1).

The office at the Eiffel Tower is open from May 1 to September 30, 11am-6pm.

There is a 24-hour information line in English, ph 49 52 53 56.

Local Transport

The first thing to do when you arrive in Paris is get hold of a copy of **Paris par Arrondissement** which has good maps of Paris, the subway system and the bus routes. It is available from bookstores and major news stands.

Buses are an economical way to get around, as 12 Francs (2 tickets) will cover the whole metropolitan area. Single tickets are available on the bus, or books of ten can be obtained from Metro stations and some tobacco shops.

The Metro (underground) can be a bit confusing at first, but if you read your map, and the maps on the street and inside the station, you will soon get the hang of it.

There are around 14,500 taxis in Paris, but as usual this is an expensive way to get around. Taxis can be hailed in the street, picked up a taxi stand, or summoned by phone.

Accommodation

Paris Hilton is a modern 5-star hotel on the Left Bank, close to the Eiffel Tower. Facilities include restaurants, bars and shops.

L'Horset Opera Hotel is 4-star hotel in the heart of Paris, close to the Opera. Facilities include a bar/lounge.

Mercure Montmartre is a 3-star hotel situated three minutes walk from the Moulin Rouge, in the fascinating Montmartre district.

Nord et D'Anvers is a 2-star hotel in the heart of the city. It has been completely renovated; facilities—a breakfast room and lounge.

There are five youth hostels in Paris:

Le D'Artagnan, 80 rue Vitruve, ph (1) 4361 0875, fax (1) 4361 7540.

Cite des Sciences, 1 Rue Jean-Baptiste Clement, ph (1) 4843 2411, fax (1) 4843 2682.

Jules Ferry, 8 Boulevard Jules Ferry, ph (1) 4357 5560.

Rue Marcel Duhamel, rue Marcel Duhamel, 91290 Arpajon, ph (1) 6490 2885.

Relais Europeen de la Jeunesse, 52 avenue Robert Schumann, 91200 Athis Mons, ph (1) 6984 8139, fax (1) 6984 7848.

Food and Drink

People have been known to visit France simply to partake of the food and wine, and if there was any time left, to take in the sights. This would be a very expensive visit, because meals in French restaurants and restaurant-bars are not cheap, in fact they are often very expensive. Nevertheless, the food is usually very good, and it goes without saying that French wine is magnifique.

All restaurants in France are required to display outside their premises a full bill of fare, with prices. It is a good idea to study this before entering, and to look for some of the *menus* or fixed-price meals. These usually offer three or four courses at a much more reasonable price than choosing from the a la carte section.

Sightseeing

Following is a walking tour of the city, which would be quite difficult to achieve in one day, but which covers all the main sights. One thing to keep in mind, Paris is not called the City of Light for nothing, and every visitor should ensure that they take a tour, grab a cab, or catch a bus at night time to see the city illuminations. An evening trip down the Avenue des Champs-Elysees is truly unforgettable.

A tour should begin where it all started .

Ile de la Cite, *the geographical centre of Paris.*

Go across the Pont d'Arcole,which spans the Seine's arm, and on the left is the **Town Hall**. In 1871 it was the barracks of the Paris Commune who fought their last battles in the 20th arrondissement. Also in the 20th arrondissement around metro Belleville and metro

PARIS

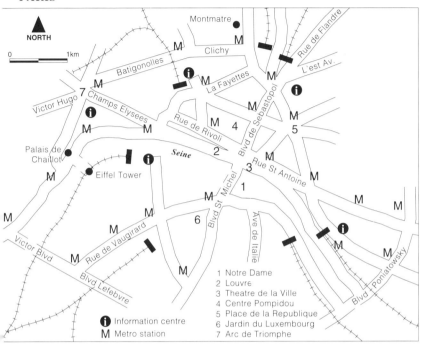

Menilmontant is the international quarter, with its worldwide charm. On the Ile de la Cite, is the cathedral of **Notre Dame**, arguably Paris's greatest and most famous building. Of French Gothic architecture, the cathedral was built between 1163 and 1345, and is one of the most beautiful churches in the world. It has an archaeological vault/tomb and museum that are well worth a visit.

Other buildings on the island are the **Palais de Justice**, the legal headquarters of France, and the **Conciergerie**, which was the "Antechamber of the Guillotine" during the Revolution. It was here that Marie-Antoinette and many others spent the night before their appointment with Madame Guillotine. Visitors can see her chapel and crucifix, a guillotine blade, Robespierre's cell and the Cour des

Femmes, where the condemned said their last farewells to their loved ones. Behind the Palais de Justice is the **Sainte-Chapelle**, which was built by St Louis (Louis IX) in 1248.

Next to the Ile de la Cite is the **Ile St Louis** which is usually overlooked, but it is where you can buy the best ice cream and sorbet, at Berthillon.

Take Pont Sully to the north bank of the Seine, then follow Boulevard Henri IV to the **Place de la Bastille**, a large square that is all that is left of the famous prison. Relatively new to this square is the **Opera de la Bastille**, which has performances for the people who live in the suburbs to the east of here. The tickets are affordable, unlike the other opera venues, and it is not necessary to dress up for the occasion.

A short walk from here is the **Place des Vosges**, which was the Place Royale. It has thirty-eight town houses built over long arcades. It has been restored, and House 6, where Victor Hugo once lived and worked, has been turned into a museum dedicated to him. Continue along rue des Francs-Bourgeois and after a few blocks the **Pompidou Centre** presents itself. It has to be one of the ugliest buildings of all time, but this in itself guarantees hundreds of visitors each day. The centre contains a library, a children's workshop, a theatre workshop, a music laboratory, and the **National Museum of Modern Art**.

The next stop is **Forum des Halles**, a vast underground complex under the Metro and RER stations. This was the site of the city's food market since the 12th century, but modern traffic and lack of space forced the market out into the suburbs (near Orly Airport). The complex is still being developed, and when completed will be a mini-city underground. The only things that remain at street level are the Fountain of the Innocents and the well-known Pied de Cochon restaurant, which is always open.

The Louvre

Walk down to rue de Rivoli, turn right, and a short way ahead is the **Palais du Louvre**.

The Louvre was a medieval fortress built in 1200 during the reign of Philippe Auguste. The site was called Lupara, and the fortress was where Paris's defences were the weakest. Now this location is at the south-west quarter of the Square Courtyard, where there are remains of several towers unearthed between 1984 and 1985. In the 14th century, Charles V added to the building and it became a royal residence, but then came the Hundred Years' War, and royalty became enamoured of the Loire valley for over 150 years, deserting their capital.

The 16th century saw Francois I demolish the keep and replace the rest with a Renaissance style building. This style of architecture was continued with additions and renovations through the various reigns. The Louvre Museum came into being at the end of the 18th century during the French Revolution, when it was decided that the royal collections should be on display for everyone.

Now the Louvre is the largest complex in Paris, and it contains the world's richest collection of art. It is impossible to see it all in one day, or even to take in what you have seen in one day, but if you are not really into art and just want a quick look-see, the following will help. The *Mona Lisa* is behind glass in the Italian Gallery; the *Winged Victory of Samothrace* and the *Venus de Milo* are in the Greek and Roman section; and Rembrandt's *Bathsheba at her Toilet* (used in magazine ads in Australia for early detection of breast cancer) is in the Dutch collection.

It is open Wed-Mon 9am-6pm, and until 10pm on Mon and Wed, and guided tours are available. Admission is 40F before 3pm, 20F after 3pm and all day Sunday, and free for the under 18s. It might be wise to mention now that there are 62 museums and monuments in Paris and the greater metropolitan area, so if you intend to visit a few it might be a good idea to enquire about the Carte Musee et Monuments pass. It is available from museums, monuments and main Metro stations, and costs 55F for one day (which would have to be a very long day to fit in several museums), 110F for three days, and 160F for five days.

Near here, along rue de Rivoli, is the Place du Palais Royal, and the **Palais Royal** itself. This was originally owned by Cardinal Richelieu, but today its arcades have shops selling all sorts of odds and ends. From the corner of the Palais the Avenue de l'Opera leads off at an angle and finishes at the Place de l'Opera and the **Opera House**, now called the Opera Paris-Garnier in honour of its architect (or one could say that somebody had to take the blame).

Meanwhile, back on the tour the next stop is the **Jardin des Tuileries**, at the east end of which is the **Arc de Triomphe du Carrousel**, a small version of the real thing. The Tuileries gardens are about 1km long, are well set out with statues, pools, fountains and playgrounds and make a very pleasant distraction from sightseeing. At the west end of the gardens, though, is the **Orangerie**, a museum devoted to the works of the Impressionists. It has two oval basement rooms covered with murals of Monet's water-lilies - incredible!

From there it is only a few steps to the **Place de la Concorde**, the central square of Paris, with its Egyptian obelisk. Now it is time to stroll down the **Champs-Elysees**, firstly past the **Grand** and **Petit Palais** (on the left) and the presidential **Palais de l'Elysee** (right), then past department stores, restaurants, cinemas, the fountains of the Rond-Point des Champs-Elysees, and finally reaching the **Place de L'Etoile** (now Place Charles de Gaulle) and the magnificent **Arc de Triomphe**.

This monument to France's military victories was conceived by Napoleon and is built on a raised platform. It is 50m high and 45m wide, and is covered with statuary and bas-reliefs denoting victories in various wars and battles. Underneath the arch is the Tomb of the Unknown Soldier from World War I, on which a flame is continually burning. It is a very moving monument, and should not be missed. There is also access to the top for fantastic views of the city.

The Champs Elysees becomes the Avenue de la Grande Armee, and then the modern **Palais de Congres** is on the right and the **Bois de Boulogne** is on the left. The Bois is a beautiful park, but not recommended at night.

From the Arc de Triomphe take Avenue Kleber to the **Palais de Chaillot**, best known for the view from there to the Eiffel Tower, but also home to the **Museum of Mankind** and the **Cinema Museum**.

The Eiffel Tower

Anyway, there it is, the **Eiffel Tower**, and as you get closer to it, and it seems to get larger, you will notice the thousands of people milling around its foundations. There are people in long queues waiting to board the elevators that take visitors up to any of the three viewing stations; there are quite a few hardy types who are starting/finishing the 1652 stairs that rise to the top station; and there quite a few who are saying, "No way. I'm not going up there, it doesn't look sturdy enough." And it does look a bit fragile, just like scaffolding.

Designed by Gustave Eiffel, and built for the World Exhibition in 1889, the tower is 300m high (the temperatures causes this figure to vary by about 40cm - higher when hotter), and the views from the stations are magnificent. The best time is supposed to be about an hour before sunset.

In front of the tower is the **Champ de Mars**, which leads to the **Hotel des Invalides**, built by Louis XIV as a hospital for 4000 war veterans. In the hospital is the **Musee de l'Armee**, probably the finest military museum in the world, and in the grounds is a Baroque domed church that contains Napoleon's tomb.

North of the City

Take the Metro to Blanche and come face to face with the famous **Moulin Rouge** complete with windmill. The area around Boulevard de Clichy and the **Place Pigalle** was made famous by Toulouse-Lautrec, and it is still the scene of the sleazy side of Paris nightlife. During the day it looks extremely tacky, but at night it does tend to take on a glamorous air. There are a few street markets that may grab the attention.

With the Moulin Rouge on the left, continue along Boulevard de Clichy to rue de Steinkerque, turn left and follow the street up to the long flight of stairs that leads to **Montmartre**. This hill has had a very long and colourful history. The Romans built a temple to the god Mercury here; in the 3rd century AD it was renamed Mont des Martyrs in honour of the execution of St Denis; in 1871 hundreds of rebels were massacred in the caves; in the late 1800s, it became an artists' colony and earned the title of the birthplace of modern art; and today it is teeming with tourists. But don't let that you put you off. The artists are still there, and you can have your portrait sketched while you wait (but settle on the price first); or you can wander around the narrow cobbled streets, visiting the art and craft shops; or you can pop into a bistro and have real French Onion Soup, which is a meal in itself. A visit to the **Basilique du Sacre-Coeur** might not be high on your list, but there is a great view of the city from the walkways around the domes.

If you decide to take the funicular down the hill, check out the souvenir shops to the right of the top station. Sometimes they have stock that is unavailable anywhere else in Paris.

Versailles

A trip to Versailles should be compulsory for every visitor who lands in Paris, and it can be reached by RER route C.

Versailles was built by Louis XIV, the Sun King, and was completed in 1682. Louis made it the official residence of the court and the seat of royal power. As the court consisted of the royal family, all their close relatives, the king's advisors, and everybody's personal servants, as well as the household staff, it is no wonder that the Palace of Versailles is so large. The western face of the building measures over 600m.

Amazingly, back in its early days the palace was open to the general public, though obviously not to the extent that it is today. Now visitors are admitted to the Sun King's private quarters above the official suite, but in those days Louis would not have appreciated a crowd dropping in (especially if he was entertaining Madame du Barry).

Versailles is open Tues-Sun 9am-6pm (May-Sept), 9am-5pm (Oct-April), ph 30 84 74 00. The park and gardens are open daily from dawn to dusk. Fireworks displays are held once a month, and the Grands Eaux (fountains display) is held on some Sundays from May to mid-October.

Attractions not to be missed are:
❏ **The Hall of Mirrors,**
❏ **The Chapel,**
❏ **The various apartments;**
❏ **The Opera Royale;**
❏ **The Grand Trianon;**
❏ **The Petit Trianon;**
❏ **and the beautiful gardens.**

Euro-Disneyland

Situated 30km east of Paris, off the A4 motorway, this theme park is a very expensive way to spend a day. It has an area of more than 2000ha, and is modelled on the original Disneyland in California. Some of the US rides have been duplicated, but they can't duplicate the continual sunshine offered by Anaheim, so the weather can cause a problem. Nevertheless, the park is attracting thousands of visitors each day, and it is wise to arrive early, or stay till the death, to avoid long queues.

Nice

Situated in the south-eastern corner of the country in the *departement* of Alpes-Maritimes, Nice is known as the Queen of the Riviera. It is a very pretty part of the world, and the departure point for trips to Corsica.

Nice is a popular holiday resort to which thousands flock every year, despite the fact that its plentiful beach is all pebbles.

History

Nice belonged to Italy until it was given to France in 1860 by the House of Savoy. It has always been a favourite with English tourists, and until World War II it had that Oh So English trademark, a long pier jutting out into the Mediterranean. Still, Nice must have appreciated this annual English influx because the waterfront street is called Promenade des Anglais.

Tourist Information

The information office is found in Avenue Thiers, at the railway station, ph 93 87 07 07.

Local Transport

There is a regular bus service from the Promenade des Anglais to the airport, and long distance buses to Cannes, Toulon and Marseille. Between Gare de Provence in Nice and Digne in the coastal alps there is a private railway - *Chemins de Fer de Provence.* It winds through the romantic Var Valley.

Accommodation

Elysees Palace is a superior first class hotel in the downtown area. Facilities include restaurant, bar, swimming pool.
West End Hotel is a superior first class hotel in the downtown area. Facilities include restaurant, bar, coffee shop and shops.
Abela, is a first class hotel in the midtown area. Facilities include restaurant, bar, disco, health club, pool and beauty salon.

There are two youth hostels in Nice:
AJ Nice, Route Forestiere du Mont Alban, ph 938 92 364, fax 920 40 310. *Summer Hostel,* for details contact the AJ Nice hostel above.

Food and Drink

The food is called Nicoise and the local specialty is bouillabaisse, that very tasty fish stew. There are many eateries within walking distance of the Promenade des Anglais, from the expensive restaurants in the first class hotels, to small coffee shops and self-service places.

Sightseeing

The **Promenade des Anglais** is 7km long, runs along the waterfront, and is lined with palm trees and flowers. It is also lined with expensive hotels, including the famous Hotel Negresco, and casinos and expensive cafes.

At the intersection of the Promenade and the Quais des Etats Unis, broad boulevards branch off to Place Massena. They are the connections between the old, or lower, part of town at the foot of Chateau Hill and the new city centre around Avenue Jean Medecin (in the direction of the railway station) and the Boulevard Victor Hugo. Then there is the harbour area, Lympia, east of the Chateau and west of Mont Boron.

In the old town area, walk along the Boulevard Jean Jaure from Promenade du Paillon to the Port Fosse steps, then turn right into rue du Marche, past the Palais de Justice, Place du Palais, to the Marche aux Fleurs (flower market) and the Fruits et Legumes (fruit and vegetable market) on Cours Saleya. The **Galerie de Malacologie** is at no. 3 Cours Saleya, and has exhibits of the fauna of the Mediterranean.

There are some beautiful buildings in the old town. At the east of the markets is a building which was the old Savoy Senate building until 1792, and later the Law Court until 1860. One street further on is **Adam and Eve House**. A little further on is the baroque **Eglise de Jesus**, and across the street of the same name is the cathedral of **St Raparate** on Place Rossetti which was named in honour of the martyr. Walk through the lanes - Halle aux Herbes, Place Entrale, rue du Collet, until you get to the rue St Augustin/rue Pairolliers - for some very picturesque old town scenery.

From here rue de la Providence climbs up to Le Chateau, a former fort, from where there are panoramic views. On the other side are: **Place Garibaldi**, an early extension of the town; the **Quai des Etats Unis** has the **Museum of Contemporary Art**; a bit further on is the **Naval Museum** in the 16th century Bellanda Tower.

There are a few interesting places to visit in the suburb of **Cimiez** - the **Archaeological Site and Museum**, with the **Matisse Museum** in the same building; and the **Marc Chagall Museum** in Avenue Dr Menard.

Principality of Monaco

To the east of Nice, further along the sea front, is the **Principality of Monaco**, a sovereign state surrounded by the *departement* of Alpes-Maritimes. It has been ruled by the Grimaldis since 1308.

Monaco consists of three parts: the capital Monaco, the resort of Monte Carlo, and the commercial centre of La Condamine - although one flows into the other and a visitor would not notice any distinct areas.

Although the name 'Monte Carlo' is almost synonymous with the word 'gambling', only a small percentage (about 3%) of Monaco's revenue comes from the casinos. But, if you are in the neighbourhood, why not try your luck? It is necessary to show your passport to participate in any gambling. If, on the other hand, you are a people watcher, grab a table in one of the outdoor places opposite the casino, and see how the other half live.

GERMANY

Kiel

Schleswig-
Holstein

Rostock

Mecklenburg-
Vorpommern

Hamburg

Bremen

Lower
Saxony

Hannover

Berlin

★

Berlin

Brandenburg

Sachsen-
Anhalt

North
Rhine-Westphalia

Lelpzlg

Sachsen

Dresden

Cologne

Bonn

Hesse

Thuringen

Rhineland-
Palatinate

Frankfurt

Saarland

Stuttgart

Bavaria

Baden-
Württemburg

Munich

Germany

The Federal Republic of Germany is situated in central Europe and has an area of 356,755 sq km. The population is 76,877,000, and the official language is German. English is taught in schools, and most people in the hospitality industry are fluent in English.

Climate

The climate is generally mild, with harsher winters in the Bavarian Alps. The July average is 21C, and the January average -1C.

Entry Regulations

Visitors must have a valid passport, and a visa is not required for visits of up to three months.

The duty free allowance is 400 cigarettes or 100 cigars or 500 gm of tobacco, 1 litre of spirits (more than 22 degrees proof) or 2 litres of spirits (up to 22 degrees proof) and 2 litres of wine. There is no restriction on the import or export of local or foreign currencies.

No vaccinations are required for any international traveller.

Currency

The currency of the land is the Deutsche Mark (DM), which is divided into 100 Pfennigs.

Approximate exchange rates, which should be used as a guide only, are:

A$	= 1DM
Can$	= 0.95DM
NZ$	= 0.85DM
S$	= 0.95DM.

UK£	= 2.20DM
US$	= 1.35DM

Notes are in denominations of 1000, 500, 200, 100, 50, 20 and 10 Deutsche Marks, and coins are 5, 2 and 1DM, and 50, 20, 10, 5, 2 and 1 Pfennigs.

Shopping hours are Mon-Fri 9am-6.30pm (Thurs until 8.30pm), Sat 9am-2pm (until 4pm on the first Sat of each month). Shops are closed on Sundays.

Credit cards are widely accepted.

Telephone

International direct dialling is available and the International code is 00, the country code 49. International calls can be made from booths marked 'Auslandsgesprache', or from post offices.

Payphones have slots for 10 Pfennigs, 1DM and 5DM, or phonecards (Telefonkarten) are available at post offices. Booths where these can be used are marked 'Kartentelefon'. Reverse charge (collect) calls can only be made to the United States.

It is very expensive to make international calls from hotels.

Driving

Germany has nearly 11,000km of toll-free motorways (autobahn), as well as highways that are famous worldwide for their scenic countryside.

UK, American and Canadian citizens can hire a car with a valid driving licence from their own country, other nationalities require an international driver's licence. Traffic drives on the right, seat belts are compulsory, and children under 12 years are not permitted to travel in the front seat.
Speed limits are:

Built-up areas	50kph,
Open roads	100kph,
Motorways	130kph.

Miscellaneous

Local time is GMT + 1, and there is daylight saving in the summer time.

Electricity - 220v AC 50 Hertz, with round ended two-pin plugs.

Health - Visitors from EC countries are covered for medical costs, but all other travellers should have health insurance.

Berlin

Berlin lies in the north German lowlands, on the banks of the Spree River, and its name comes from a Slovakian word meaning 'built on a marsh'. The city has an area of 892 sq km, and it is the third largest in Europe (only London and Paris are larger). It measures 45km from east to west and 38km from north to south, and is divided into 23 districts, each one a city in itself. The population is around 3.5 million.

Although the Wall came down in 1990, Berliners still think of themselves as either Ossis (East) or Wessis (West), as a large proportion cannot remember life before the Wall.

History

History first records Berlin as a city in 1251, in competition with the city of Colln, on the left bank of the Spree. The two cities combined in 1307, under the name of Berlin.

Berlin has had a colourful history ever since the elector of Brandenburg made it his official residence in 1447. It was involved in the Thirty Years War that began in 1618, was invaded by Napoleon in 1806, warred with Austria in 1866, and France in 1870, and was made the capital city of the German Empire in 1871. In 1914, the first world war commenced when Germany invaded France, and in 1918 it concluded with Germany's defeat. Kaiser Wilhelm II abdicated, and the same year the Weimar Republic was established.

1933 saw Hitler elected, and under his leadership Germany

headed for the second world war, invading Poland in 1939. Once again Germany was defeated, and in 1945 the allied armies entered Berlin and divided it into four sectors.

The communist DDR (German Democratic Republic) built the Wall in 1961, dividing Berlin into East and West. After the demolition of the wall, all-German elections were held in 1990 and the Christian Democrat coalition was voted into power. Berlin once again became the seat of parliament in 1991.

Tourist Information

The Berlin Tourist Office has several branches: on the ground floor of the Europa Center, Budapester Strasse entrance, and they are open Mon-Sat 8am-10.30pm, Sun 9am-9pm, ph 262 6031; Tegel Airport Main Hall, open daily 8am-11pm, ph 41 01 31 45; Bahnhof Zoo, open Mon-Sat 8am-11pm, ph 313 9063-64; Brandenburg Gate, open daily 8am-8pm, ph E/212-4675.

The Berlin Information Centre, Hardenbergstrasse 20, 1000 Berlin 12, ph 31 00 40, has plenty of free maps and brochures.

Local Transport

Public transport in Berlin consists of the U-Bahn (underground), S-Bahn trains, single and double-decker buses. The East is serviced by trams.

Unfortunately, using the underground system in the city is confusing and time consuming, with several transfers often necessary to get from A to B. Many U-Bahn stations are inundated with signs that only add to the confusion, as they tell of transfers, exits, transit directions, but there is a shortage of signs telling travellers where they are. Also, there are few stations that have local maps to aid orientation.

Electric **trams** were invented in Berlin, with the first one going into service in 1881. The trams in East Berlin have rattly old carriages, but those in Potsdam are in good repair. Tram stops have HH signs.

Buses can be just as confusing as the underground, but if you enjoy the double-decker variety, why not try to come to grips with the system. **Remember the front stairs are for going up, the back for going down.** Bus stops have a green H on them.

There are different kinds of reduced fare tickets available

from ticket offices or, more conveniently, from machines.

A tip for finding your way around Berlin: street numbers run up one side of a street, then down the other, so that no. 2 may be opposite no. 300, depending on the length of the street. The street numbers for each block are indicated on signs on street corners.

Accommodation

As mentioned previously, Berlin is a big city, so you can expect to find plenty of accommodation. Following are a few of the inner city accommodation outlets, with prices in DM that should be used as a guide only.

Alsterhof Ringhotel Berlin, Augsburger Strasse 5, ph 21 24 20 - 300 beds - restaurant, bar, indoor swimming pool - 290-390DM including buffet breakfast.

Hotel Am Zoo, Kurfurstendamm 25, ph 8 84 37-0 - 198 beds - bar - 316-386DM including buffet breakfast.

Art Hotel Sorat, Joachimstaler Strasse 29, ph 88 44 70 - 150 beds - restaurant, bar - 270-290DM.

Best Western Hotel Boulevard, Kurfurstendamm 12, ph 88 42 50 - 114 beds - bar - 260-350DM.

Berlin Plaza Hotel, Knesebeckstrasse 63, ph 88 00 2-0 - 221 beds - restaurant, bar - 198-335DM including buffet breakfast.

Hotel Berliner Hof, Tauentzienstrasse 8, ph 2 62 30 61 - 80 beds - 190-310DM including buffet breakfast.

Food and Drink

Traditional Berlin fare, such as blockwurst and meat balls, is in small supply, but there are still a few places that stick with the originals. Here is a selection.

Wilhelm Hoeck, Charlottenburg, Wilmersdorfer Strasse 149, ph 3 41 81 74 - open Mon-Sat 8am-midnight. Home made meat rissoles, gherkins and pickled eggs near the draught beer taps. This is as old Berlin as you can get.

Laternchen, Charlottenburg, Windscheidstrasse 24, ph 3 24 68 82 - open Mon-Fri 6pm-midnight, Sat-Sun 6pm-1am. The decor is definitely Old Berlin, but sometimes the menu can have a few imports.

Marjellchen, Charlottenburg, Mommsenstrasse 9, ph 8 83 26 76 - open Mon-Sat noon-midnight, Sun 5pm-midnight. Believed by some to have the best Konigsberg dumplings in town, this eatery also has alcoholic Danzig Goldwasser on offer.

Zur letzten Instanz, Mitte, Waisenstrasse 14-16, ph 2 42 55 28 - open daily noon-1am. This is one of, if not the oldest pub in Berlin, dating back to 1621. In keeping with this reputation there is always "Eisbein" (pickled pork shank) on the menu.

Germans are great beer-drinkers, so it is not difficult to locate a pub, in fact there seems to be one on every corner.

Shopping

The best known department store in Berlin is the Kaufhaus des Westens, better known as KaDeWe, in Wittenbergplatz. It opened in 1907, and is the largest department store in Germany, and the third largest in Europe - Galeries Lafayette in Paris is the largest, followed by Harrods in London.

KaDeWe has seven floors, but it is the sixth floor that almost puts the store in the sightseeing category, for this is where the legendary giant delicatessen is found.

The Europa Centre at Breitscheidplatz has a shopping centre, and shopping streets are: Kurfurstendamm and its side streets; Schloss Strasse in Steglitz; Wilmersdorfer Strasse in Charlottenburg; Savignyplatz; Savignybogen; and Under den Linden between Brandenburger Tor and Alexanderplatz.

Forms for reclaiming VAT are issued with the purchase, and the refund is issued on leaving Germany.

Sightseeing

Charlottenburg

The centre of unified Berlin is in the district of Charlottenburg, and this is the best place to begin a tour.

The **Kaiser-Wilhelm-Gedachtniskirche** (Emperor William Memorial Church) on Breitscheidplatz, ph 24 50 23, was almost completely destroyed during World War II, due to its proximity to the strategically important Zoo station. The powers that be wanted to raze the ruins, but Berlin magazines aroused public interest in the project and a new complex has risen from the ashes. Guided tours are available on Thurs and Fri at 1.15pm, 3pm and 4.30pm, and it is worth visiting for the beautiful mosaic ceiling in the small hall. This is as beautiful as the original church, which is not what some think about the rest of the building.

Kurfurstendamm, affectionately called Ku'damm, branches off opposite the church. This street is 3.5km long and 60m wide, and Otto von Bismarck, the first German chancellor, decided to make it into a shopping and amusement avenue. Apparently he had become enamoured of the Champs Elysees during a trip to Paris in 1871, and wanted to make the Ku'damm as famous, if not more so. All buildings were to be four storeys, and the facades had to be decorated with stucco. English gardens were to be laid out in the front of the houses, and those on the corners had to have a dome on top. It was magnificent but, unfortunately, World War II destroyed 202 of the original 250 buildings.

Fasanenstrasse runs off Ku'damm, and at no. 79-80 is the Judisches Gemeindehaus (Jewish Community House), ph 883 65 48. This modern center for Berlin's 6000 Jews was built on the foundations of a Byzantine synagogue that was burned to the ground on infamous Kristallnacht, November 9, 1938. The present building has fragments of the former portal in the entrance. A bronze sculpture by Richard Hess stands in front of the building and has an inscription from the book of Moses.

Back on Breitscheidplatz is the **Europa Centre**, the building with the Mercedes symbol on the top. This twenty-three storey building has more than one hundred shops and restaurants, a casino, La Vie en Rose nightclub, the Tourist Office and various airline offices. A **Panoramic Lookout** is a few steps up from the 22nd floor, and access is on Tauentzienstrasse between the Dresdner Bank and the cinema. This tower is open daily 9am-midnight, and admission is DM3, but it is worth it on a clear day.

The Europa Centre stands where the famous Romanische Cafe stood before it was destroyed in the war.

Opposite the Europa Centre and the Memorial Church is the **State Art Gallery**, which is sometimes used for exhibitions.

The **Bahnhof Zoo** (Zoo Train Station) was completely

renovated for the 750th anniversary of Berlin in 1987. It is both a mainline and S-Bahn station as well as a U-Bahn station in the annex. The station has an information counter, a hotel reservation display, a bookstore and lockers, and because it is in the middle of the zoo complex, every other kind of shop is in close vicinity.

The **Zoologistche Garten** (Zoo) is across from the station in Hardenbergplatz, ph 25 40 10, and it is open daily 9am-sunset. Home to 10,000 animals, this zoo claims to have more species than any other. Admission is DM7. When Berlin was a divided city a second zoo was established in Friedrichsfelde, the **Tierpark**. It is not as large as the West Berlin establishment, but it does have the largest polar bear collection in the world.

While at the zoo you might consider visiting the **Aquarium** which is in the building next to the Elephant Gate. Admission is DM7, or you can get a combined zoo/aquarium ticket for DM11.

From the Zoo underground station take a train to either Sophie-Charlotte Platz, or the more convenient Richard-Wagner Platz, then follow the signs to the **Charlottenburg Palace** (Schloss), the most beautiful baroque building in Berlin.

Charlottenburg Palace

Originally built as an eleven window summer house for Sophie Charlotte, the wife of the future King Friedrich I, it was completed in its present form, with the cream-coloured facade measuring 505m, in 1790.

The palace was severely damaged during the bombing raids of World War II, but there has been much careful restoration. The gardens were originally in the French style, but in the early 19th century they were remodelled into a somewhat disorganised English style. The most recent restoration has preserved the best of both. Interesting buildings in the park include the **Schinkel Pavilion**, a Neapolitan style villa built by Friedrich Wilhelm III and his second wife Princess Liegnitz. It is open Tues-Sun 10am-5pm, and admission is 2.50DM. Near the banks of the Spree, at the north of the park is the **Belvedere**, built in 1788 as a teahouse for Friedrich Wilhelm II. It is open Tues-Sun 10am-5pm, and admission is also 2.50DM.

At the end of a line of fir trees on the west side of the park is the **Mausoleum**, open Tues-Sun 10am-5pm, admission 2.50DM. This temple was built by Friedrich Wilhelm III for his Queen Liuse. Several other royals have been interred here.

The **Historical Rooms** (Historische Raume) of the Palace are open to the general public Tues-Sun 10am-5pm, Thurs until 8pm, and admission for all buildings and rooms is 6DM. This is another opportunity to see how royalty spent their waking and sleeping moments, but don't expect this tour to be another Versailles.

The **Orangerie** at the west end of the palace was built as a hothouse, became a theatre during the late 1780s, and is now a coffee shop.

Museums
Whilst in this area there are a few museums to visit. The **Egyptian Museum**, 70 Schloss Strasse, ph 32 09 11, was built as barracks for the royal bodyguards. It now has one of the best Egyptian collections in the world, with two really outstanding pieces - a 3400-year-old bust of the beautiful Nefertiti, wife of Pharaoh Akhenaton, from the Tel el-Amarna period; and the Kalabasha Monumental Gate built around 20BC for the Roman Emperor Augustus. The latter was presented to the museum by the Egyptian government when its site was flooded by the Aswan High Dam; the former was unearthed by a team of German archaeologists in 1912, and, like so many of Egypt's treasures, was "souvenired".

Across from this building is the **Antikenmuseum**, ph 32 09 11, with a good collection of ancient Greek, Etruscan and Roman art, and the Treasury in the basement has a silver and gold collection dating from around 2000BC.

The **Brohan Museum** is opposite the Palace, ph 321 4029, and is open Tues-Sun 10am-6pm, Thurs till 8pm. It has a large collection of Art Deco paintings, sculptures, arts and crafts and furniture, collected between 1889 and 1939.
Admission is DM3.

In Sophie-Charlotte Strasse, no. 17-18 is the **Plaster Cast House**, ph 321 7011, open Mon-Fri 9am-4pm, Wed till 6pm. A bit different from ordinary museums, this is a branch of the Prussian Cultural Foundation, and visitors can buy plaster casts of about 7000 of the foundation's exhibits (even including Nefertiti).

Heading away from Charlottenburg, travel along Otto-Suhr Allee to Ernst Reuter Platz, named for the first mayor of Berlin after the second world war, then on to Strasse des 17 Juni, which bisects the **Technical University**. Follow this street to the **Charlottenburger Tor**, over the Landwehr Canal. This was the entrance to Charlottenburg from the Tiergarten district, and was built in 1905, the 200th anniversary of the death of Sophie Charlotte. On the left of the gate is Friedrich I (originally Elector Friedrich III), and on the right is his wife Sophie Charlotte, pointing the way to the Palace. The original gate was larger than at present because in 1937, the size of the columns was reduced to enable Hitler's architect Speer to have enough room for his grand avenue for Nazi victory parades - Charlottenburger Chaussee. The present name of the street is derived from the workers' uprising in East Berlin on June 17, 1953.

Brandenburger Tor

Probably the best way to get to the gate from Charlottenburger is to catch double-decker Bus 100, which begins its journey in front of *McDonald's* at the Zoo train station. Although this is a normal part of the local transport system, it has become tops with sightseers as its route takes in all the important attractions between east and west. The fact that it only costs DM2 has probably added to its popularity.

The first stop is the Europa Center, then the bus makes its way to Spreeweg, and the stop marked **Grosser Stern** (Big Star). This large roundabout has a **Victory Monument** which can be climbed for a good view of the surrounding area. The bus then continues past Schloss Bellevue, along John Foster Dulles Allee, for a stop in front of the **Kongresshalle** (locally called the Pregnant Oyster, for obvious reasons). The next stop is the Reichstag, then Reichstag Sud (south) in front of the Gate, then past what was the Wall, then a left turn onto **Unter den Linden** (under the lime trees), probably the best-known street in Berlin.

The first Brandenburg Gate was part of the walls of the old city, and it was demolished in 1788. The present gate was opened on August 6, 1791, and it is 65.5m wide, 11m thick and 26m high. The central opening is 5.5m and was originally reserved for the use of royal coaches. The 6m quadriga, drawn by four horses, was built in 1794. Originally the winged charioteer was the Greek goddess of peace, Irene. In October 1806, Napoleon took the complete quadriga to Paris, and when it was returned in 1814, the driver had become Victoria, the victory goddess, and she had a laurel wreath and an iron cross. The quadriga was destroyed in World War II, and the East Berlin magistrate had a replica erected in 1958.

Another interesting building in this area is the **Reichstag,** built between 1884 and 1894 as the seat of the German parliament. During World War II it was almost completely ruined, and it stayed that way until the 1960s when the West German parliament decided to rebuild it as a symbol of the desire to reunite the country. There are guided tours daily at 2pm, and an audio tour for 2DM.

Outside Berlin

Potsdam
The city of Potsdam is south-west of Berlin, and begins across the Glienicke Bridge.

It is the capital city of the state of Brandenburg, and home to a world-famous tourist attraction, the **Sanssouci Palace**.

Built between 1745 and 1747 for the Prussian King Friedrich II, nicknamed "the Great", the then twelve room castle was used as a summer residence. Friedrich liked to model himself on Louis XIV, the Sun King, so French was often spoken in his court, and one of his courtiers suggested the name 'Sans souci' (French for 'without care') for his new palace.

In 1763-64, after the seven-year war, King Friedrich oversaw the building of the Neues Palais, the Picture Gallery, the New Chambers and the Chinese Teahouse, gathering a lot of his ideas from the Palace of Versailles.

Between 1851 and 1861, Friedrich Wilhelm IV decided to extend the complex, and he was influenced by anything Italian, so his buildings - the Great Orangerie, Charlottenhof Palace and the Roman Baths - reflect this different style.

Whether or not it compares with Versailles is up to each visitor to decide, and unfortunately, entry is not always guaranteed, as curators fear the damage that crowds can inflict on the buildings. As tour groups are given priority, the best thing independent travellers can do is to arrive early, pick up a numbered card, tour the gardens, then return in the afternoon to tour the palace complex.

The opening times are:
Sanssouci Castle, New Chambers, New Palace, Chinese Tea House, Charlottenhof Castle, Roman Baths -

February - September	9am-5pm
October	9am-4pm
November-January	9am-3pm
(Lunch break:	*12.30pm-1pm)*

Closed every 1st and 3rd Monday of the month.
Ladies' Wing and Orangerie Castle the middle of May to the middle of October only.

Admission:
from 3DM (Ladies' Wing) to 8DM (Sanssouci).
Note: some parts may only be visited with a guide.

To get there by car:
Autobahn Berliner Ring, Bundes-strasse 1 or 273.

By train:
Regional train R3 to Potsdam Kaiserbahnhof. S-Bahn from Berlin to Potsdam Stadt, then by tram to Luisenplatz, or the Bus line A to Sanssouci.
For further information contact Stiftung Schlosser and Garten Potsdam Sanssouci, ph 03 31/9694-0,
Visitor's service -200 and -201

Austria: Tirol area, village of Kitzbuehel in Winter

Munich: Marienplatz

West Germany: Cologne's Hohe Strasse

Bonn

In the days of The Wall and a divided country, Bonn was the capital of West Germany and the seat of government. Now it is now longer a centre of power, and has reverted to being simply the birthplace of Beethoven.

Bonn sits on the west bank of the Rhine River, approximately 30km south of Cologne.

History

Called Castra Bonnensia by the Romans when they had a full-strength legionary post on the site, Bonn was the residence of the Prince-Bishops of Cologne for about five hundred years.

During the Napoleonic era the city was occupied by his armies, and after his defeat it became part of Prussia in 1815. Shortly after this the University came into being.

Before the second world war Bonn was a quiet, attractive university town, but during the war the town centre was heavily bombed and suffered almost complete destruction. In 1949 Bonn was made the seat of the Federal Government, which caused its population to double. The town has been almost completely restored in the post war period.

Tourist Information

The Tourist Information Centre, Cassius-Bastei, Munster- strasse 20, D-5300 Bonn, ph (0228) 773 466, is open Mon-Sat 8am-9pm (April-October), Mon-Sat 8am-7pm (November- March), Sun and public holidays 9.30am-12.30pm

There is a branch of the German National Tourist Office at Niebuhrstrasse 16b, ph (0228) 214 071-72.

Sightseeing

Most of the old town is a pedestrian zone enclosed by a ring road, and the centre is the **Marktplatz**, a triangular-shaped area that has on one corner the 18th century **Town Hall**. An annex of the town hall can be entered from Rathausgasse, and it contains the city's **art collection**.

Beethoven's Birthplace

From the western corner of Marktplatz, Bonn-gasee branches off, and at no. 20 is the **Beethovenhaus** where the great composer was born in 1770. The house is now a museum dedicated to Beethoven and has been completely restored. It is open Mon-Sat 10am-5pm, Sun 10am-1pm.

South-west of the Marktplatz is the **Munster St Martin**, in Munsterplatz. A Romanesque style basilica of the 12th-13th century, the church is worth visiting for its original wall paintings. Take Remisius-strasse which runs off Munsterplatz, then turn right into Furstenstrasse and continue to Am Hof, part of the ring road. Opposite are the main buildings of the **Friedrich Wilhelms Universitat**, the university of Bonn. These buildings formed the residential palace of the Prince-Electors of Cologne.

South-west of the Munster is the main railway station, and not far from there, at 14-16 Colmantstrasse, is the **Rheinisches Landesmuseum**. It has a good collection of sculptures, paintings and antiquities, and is open Tues, Thurs 9am-5pm, Wed 9am-8pm, Fri 9am-4pm, Sat-Sun 11am-5pm.

Most of the important government buildings, including the home of the President of the Federal Republic, are in Adenauerallee. It runs parallel to, but not alongside, the Rhine.

Bad Godesberg, about 7km to the south, is a spa resort and home to several diplomatic missions. It can be reached by rail or by the B9 road. The town dates back to Roman times, but its dubious claim to fame is that it was where Adolf Hitler and Neville Chamberlain, the then Prime Minister of Britain, met in 1938 to discuss the fate of Czechoslovakia. While in Bad Godesberg, look out for Godesburg, a ruined 13th century castle that has been restored as a hotel.

Cologne (Köln)

Cologne is on the left bank of the Rhine, 40km south of Dusseldorf, and is over 2000 years old. Cologne was badly damaged during World War II, but most of the very old buildings have been carefully restored.

Many people visit Cologne during *Fastelovend* (Carnival) which begins on New Year's Eve and continues until the Monday before Ash Wednesday! Originally held to celebrate the end of winter it is now more of a time to let your hair down, with more than 300 balls held during the festival. It climaxes with a procession on Rosenmontag (Rose Monday).

History

Cologne was founded by the Romans in 38BC, and many remains from this period are still in situ. The cultural and commercial capital of the Rhineland, Cologne was guaranteed an important part in world affairs, because of its strategic position where the trade routes from the four compass points met. Today it is well known world-wide for its trade fairs, something of a carryover from the markets of earlier times.

Tourist Information

There is a very helpful information office opposite the cathedral at Untere Fettenhenen 9, D-5000, Koln 1, ph 0221 2 21 33 45.

Local Transport

The widely spread network of U-Bahn (underground), trams and buses that connect with the S-Bahn (city train) traffic of the Ruhr network, gives optimal public transport coverage.

Accommodation

Mercure Severinshof is a first class hotel in the downtown area. Facilities include restautant, bar and health club.

There are two youth hostels in Cologne:

Deutz, Siegestrasse 5a, ph (221) 814 711, fax (221) 884 425.

Riehl Jugendgastehaus, An der Schanz 14, ph (221) 767 081, fax (221) 761 555.

Food and Drink

Surprisingly, because Cologne is set on a river famous for its wines, the city has some of the best local beer in Germany, called Kolsch (which means 'belonging to Koln').

There is no special dish that is associated with Cologne, but you can be guaranteed a hearty meal in any establishment serving local food, rather than international.

Sightseeing

The obvious place to begin a tour is the **Cathedral** (Dom). Work on the building began in 1248, but it was not completed until 1842. Fortunately, though, no one lost the plans because the Gothic style was carried through to the end. During World War II, 90 per cent of the old town area was destroyed, but the Cathedral, though sustaining much damage, was still standing.

The inside of the church is very peaceful, even though it is in the middle of the hustle and bustle of the city. There is a viewing platform 97m above the city in the south tower, but there are 509 steps to be dealt with to get there. Many works of art are to be found inside, among them a wooden crucifix carved in 969, the Bible window in the choir, the Shrine of the Magi which is said to hold relics of the Three Kings, a mosaic floor in the choir. The cathedral treasury is also worth a visit.

The main railway station (hauptbahnhoff) of the city is centred next to the Dom. This area is a transport hub for the city.

The square building on the left, facing the cathedral's east end, is the **Romisch-Germanisches Museum**, which was built over the Roman Dionysus Mosaic. The mosaic was found when workmen were excavating to build an air-raid shelter during the second world war. The museum has many other exhibits of life in Cologne from Roman times to the reign of Charlemagne.

Along Unter Goldschmied strasse is a 100m long Roman drainage channel that you can walk along (the new Town Hall is also here), and the remains of the Roman town wall around the corner of Komodien and Tunis strasses and the corner of Zeughaus and Auf dem Berlich strasses. On the left of the new **Town Hall** is the centre of the old town, which is a pedestrian zone, and nearby is **St Martin's Church** which is surrounded by new buildings that blend in with the old (an early example of the present day interest in preserving the past). This part of the old town is the Alter Markt (old market) and there are several ale houses and eateries in and around, such as Papa Joe's Biersalon, Alter Markt 50-52, where non-traditional New Orleans jazz features, and the Gaffelhaus traditional restaurant at Alter Markt 20-22. Then head for Heumarkt (Haymarket), and at no. 60 there is Altstadt Paffgen, where you can grab a bite to eat, and maybe try some of the Kolsch beer.

Take Gurzenichstrasse from Heumarkt, then turn right into Unter Goldschmied and you will see the **Gurzenich**, a Gothic festival hall that was completed in 1444, and rebuilt after the second world war. From here take Obenmarspforte to Hohe strasse, a pedestrian mall that leads back towards the cathedral.

Alternatively, stay on Obenmarspforte until you reach the Offenbachplatz, then take special notice of the large Renaissance style building, or more importantly, its street number - 4711. This is where the chemist who produced the formula for Kolnisch Wasser, or as it is better known, Eau de Cologne, lived. The house is now a perfume museum, and it has an interesting clock that puts on a performance every hour from 9am to 9pm.

The streets in Koln or Cologne, however you want to pronounce it, are fairly wide and graced with many trees. An efficient tram service operates throughout the city, and the local people are most helpful in the main in giving directions.

For attractions further afield, the northern edge of the city has the Zoological Gardens and Aquarium, and in summer an aerial cableway operates across the Rhine from the zoo, offering fantastic views of the city and the cathedral. Next to the zoo is the Botanical Gardens.

Frankfurt/Main

The city of Frankfurt is situated at the crossroads of Germany. It has a population of 625,000 and is one of the world's great financial centres.

Most of the old part of the city was destroyed by bombing during the second world war, so much of what is seen now is not original.

Tourist Information

Information centres are found at: the main railway station, opposite track 23 - open November-March Mon-Sat 8am-9pm, Sun 9.30am-8pm (April-October Mon-Sat 8am-10pm, Sun 9.30am-8pm) ph (212) 38 849; Romerberg 27 - open Mon-Fri 9am-7pm, Sat and public holidays 9.30am-6pm, ph (212) 38 708.

Local Transport

Frankfurt has rail, underground, bus and tram services, with the latter being the most efficient way of getting around the city.

Accommodation

Arabella Congress is a first class hotel in the midtown area. Facilities include restaurant, bar, coffee shop, health club, swimming pool and shops.

Dorint Neiderard is a first class hotel in the midtown area. Facilities include restaurant, bar, coffee shop, health club and swimming pool.

Scandic Crown Offenbach is a first class hotel in the midtown area. Facilities include restaurant, coffee shop and swimming pool.

Frankfurt's youth hostel is

Haus der Jugend, Deutscherrnufer 12, ph (69) 619 058, fax (69) 618 257.

There are many 2 and 3 star hotels around the Hauptbanhoff such as the Metropole, Excelsior and others. Across from the Hauptbanhoff you enter the red light district very soon, so seek advice from your travel agent as to where the accommodation is positioned in the city. Depending on what time of year the prices vary considerably. Best to buy through a tour operator before departure.

You can organise private accommodation at the Messe which is the main reason why a lot of people from overseas visit Frankfurt during the year.

Accommodation Service - Messe Frankfurt GmbH Fax (69) 7575-6352, Torhaus Service Centre, level 3.

Telephone for enquiries not for reservations:

Hotel Accommodation: Ph. 7575-6222, 7575-6695

Private Accommodation: Ph. 7575-6296, 7575-6696

The Frankfurt Buchmesse hosts some 50,000 publishers and allied personnel in early October for one week each year. Avoid seeking accommodation in Frankfurt at this time.

Food and Drink

In the district of Sachsenhausen apple cider is sold at the world famous Apfelweinlokale. This area of Frankfurt is dotted with many restaurants.

Around the Opera House and along the main avenues there are some excellent restaurants. Across the river along Gartenstrasse, and around the Dom (old Cathedral - recently restored) and Town Hall (Romer) there are some delightful restaurants. Many people gravitate to the ubiquitous McDonalds, and Movenpic are also well represented in Frankfurt.

Sightseeing

Frankfurt's favourite son is Johann Wolfgang von Goethe, the famous author, and he was baptised in **Katharinekirche**, which is opposite the **Hauptwache** (Guard House), a junction for the above ground and underground rail systems. The Guard House was built in 1730, and is a good place to begin a tour of the city.

There are a couple of other churches in this vicinity - the **Liebfrauenkirche** and the **Paulskirche**. St Paul's was built 1789-1833, but was burnt to the ground in 1944. Because of its historical significance as the meeting place of the German

National Assembly in the 1840s, people from all over the country donated the money to have it rebuilt.

Not far from St Paul's, at 23 Grosser Hirschgraben, is **Goethehaus**, where the great man was born and lived. It is now a museum, and is open Mon-Sat 9am-6pm, Sun 10am-1pm (April-September); Mon-Sat 9am-4pm, Sun 10am-1pm (October-March).

On the nearby Romerberg is the city's restored landmark - the Romer, the town hall complex of buildings. Of them, the **Kaidersaal** (Imperial Hall) in the Zum Romer is open to the public Mon-Sat 9am-5pm, Sun 10am-4pm. The tourist information office is at Romerberg 27, and they have good free maps of the city.

To the left of the Romer is the **Imperial Cathedral** (Kaiserdom), where the German emperors were elected and crowned. The building is from the 14th-15th centuries, and has many works of art including a life-size stone Calvary scene by Hans Backoffen (1509).

From here head towards the river and the **Historisches Museum**, with a varied collection that includes a model of Frankfurt of 1912 and replicas of the crown jewels of the Holy Roman Empire. The museum is open Tues 10am-5pm, Wed 10am-8pm, Thurs-Sat 10am-5pm, and there is no general admission fee.

Other Museums
On the other side of the river from here are seven museums. The **Museum of Arts and Crafts** (Museum fur Kunsthandwerk) has four sections - Far Eastern, European, Islamic, and books and writing. It is open Tues-Sun 10am-5pm, Wed until 8pm, and admission is free.

The **Ethnological Museum** (Museum fur Volkerkunde) has a very large collection from the world over. It is open Tues-Sun 10am-5pm, Wed until 8pm, and admission is free.

The **German Film Museum** (Deutsches Filmmuseum) has a good exhibition of cinematographic history. It is open Tues-Sun 11am-6.30pm and admission is free. In the lower ground floor there is a very good cafe.

The **German Architectural Museum** (Deutsches Architekturmuseum) is the only one of its kind in the world, and is only of interest to people involved, or interest in the profession. It is open Tues-Sun 10am-5pm, Wed until 8pm, and admission is free.

The **Postal Museum** (Bundespostmuseum) is only for people with special interests. It is also open Tues-Sun 11am-5pm, Wed until 8pm. Admission is free.

The **Art Institute** (Stadelsches Kunstinstitut) has a collection of 13th to 20th century art that includes works by Rubens, Durer, Rembrandt and Botticelli. It is the only museum in the group to charge admission. Open Tues-Sun 11am-5pm, Wed until 8pm.

Liebighaus is a sculpture museum with exhibits dating back to 3000BC.

These museum are only a 15 minute walk from the old centre of Town. A footbridge across the Main near the old centre of town brings you to the museum area in no time. On the Museum side there is a very pleasant walk along the river bank.

Places Further Afield

Frankfurt has a very modern **Zoo** that can be reached by the underground. The main entrance on Alfred-Brehm-Platz is open daily March 16 to September 30 daily 8am-7pm; October 1 to October 15 daily 8am-6pm; February 16 to March 15 8am-6pm. The entrance on Rhonstrasse is open daily September 16 to March 15 8am-7pm; March 16 to September 15 8am-6pm.

The **Palmengarten** is to the north of the city and has entrances on Siesmayerstrasse, Bockenheimer Landstrasse, Palmengartenstrasse, Siesmayerstrasse and Zeppelinallee. It has a large greenhouse that simulates tropical jungle conditions; other greenhouses containing tropical and sub-tropical plants; a children's playground; a train ride; and a restaurant. It is open daily Jan-Feb 9am-4pm, March 9am-5pm, April-Sept 9am-6pm, Oct 9am-5pm, Nov-Dec 9am-4pm, and there is an admission fee.

The town of **Darmstadt** is south of Frankfurt on the Bundesstrasse 3, and it was home to Hesses' grand dukes until 1918. The town's **Castle** was modelled on Versailles and is worth a visit. In the castle museum is the *Darmstadter Madonna* painted by Hans Holbein in 1526, and the Porcelain Museum has the grand dukes' collection of 18th and 19th century porcelain and earthenware.

Another attraction in the town is the **Mathildenhohe**, an artists' colony started by the last grand duke, Ernst-Ludwig. It has several interesting buildings including the Russian Chapel, built in 1899 as a present from Czar Nicholas II to his wife Alexandra, and the Marriage Tower, built in 1905. Alternatively, you can go to the university (1386 founded) town of **Heidelberg** for the day by car. Situated on the River Neckar. Recommended.

Munich

Munich, the largest city in, and capital of, Bavaria, is a very interesting place to visit that is often overlooked by visitors to Germany. Not only does it have some very interesting attractions of its own, it is a good starting point for exploring the Bavarian Alps.

History

Bavaria was an independent state for centuries before it became part of the German Empire in 1871. Bavaria had been ruled for over 700 years by the Wittelsbach family, who had overseen the town plan of Munich and had many fine buildings erected.

Even in the 1990s, the people of this area think of themselves first as Bavarians, then as Germans.

Tourist Information

There is a tourist information office at the southern exit of the main railway station, in the Bayerstrasse, opposite platform 11, ph (089) 239 1256-57, that is open Mon-Sat 8am-11pm, Sun 1-9.30pm; and another at the Town Hall in the Marienplatz.

A monthly brochure called *Der Monat in Munchen* has what's on where in the entertainment world.

Local Transport

Munich has an excellent public transport system that incorporates train, underground, trams and buses. It is best to enquire at one of the information offices about timetables and methods of buying tickets and passes. There are plenty of ticket machines available, but these can be difficult to use if you don't understand the instructions, so get that advice.

Food and Drink

Bavarians eat a great deal of pork, so you won't see much in the way of beef or lamb dishes on the menu, but liberal use of the word 'schweine'. Also there will be more dumplings (which are rather delicious, although fattening) than potatoes. Sausages are a German favourite and the one associated with Munich is the Weisswurst, literally white sausage. It is made from a mixture of bacon and veal, parsley and pepper, and should be eaten with a sweet mustard.

The traditional Bavarian drink is beer, which comes in helles (light) or dunkels (dark). Special, stronger brews are made for special occasions, for example the Oktoberfest. If you can't stand the strong stuff, the word for 'shandy' is 'Radler'.

Sightseeing

A walking tour can start from the railway station.
Go along the extension of the platforms to the pedestrian zone, Schutzenstrasse, then Neuhauser Strasse and **St Michael's Church** (Michaelskirche). It is built in the Renaissance style, and is the crypt of the Wittelsbach family. The crypt is open Mon-Fri 10am-1pm, 2-4pm, Sat 10am-3pm.

Next stop is the **Frauenkirche**, the cathedral, which dates from the 15th century. It has twin towers capped with copper domes that are a city landmark, and the southern one can be climbed. It is only open from April to October, Mon-Sat 10am-5pm, and is worth the effort for the great views.

Nearby is **Marienplatz**, the centre of the city since its foundation in 1158. Here is the 15th century **Old Town Hall** (Rathaus) and the beautiful, Gothic-revival, 19th century **New Town Hall**, which has a mechanical show (automata) in the clock tower at

11am each day, and from May to October also at noon, 5pm and 9pm. The tower of the new town hall is open Mon-Fri 8.30am-7pm, Sat-Sun 10am-7pm in summer and daily 9am-4.30pm in winter.

On the right, in Rindermarkt, is the **Peterskirche** (St Peter's), the oldest and most loved church in Munich. The tower called Alter Peter can be climbed and is open Mon-Sat 9am-4pm, Sun 11am-4pm.

Keep left from here and you will come to the **Victualienmarkt**, the largest food and vegetable market. From here you can go two ways. Either keep going along Rosen Tal Strasse to the **Stadt Museum** on St Jakobs Plats (open Tues-Sun 9am-4.30pm), and then visit the **Asamkirche** in Sendinger Strasse, with its Bavarian Rococo creations, then along the Ring to Sendingertor Platz.

OR, go in the opposite direction along Sparkassen Strasse and on the right is the square with the famous **Hofbrauhaus**.

On the left is the **Alter Hof**, the first residence of the Wittelsbach rulers. Further along is Max Joseph Platz, with the **Nationaltheatre** (Opera House) and the **Residenz**, a complex of buildings that has grown over the centuries. Courtyards link the various buildings which include the **Residenzmuseum** with its fine art collection. It is open Tues-Sat 10am-4.30pm, Sun 10am-1pm. On the left is the **Feldherrnhalle**, built by Ludwig I in 1844 and copied from the Loggia dei Lanzi in Florence. And behind here on Odeons Platz is the **Theatinerkirche**, with its impressive dome and towers.

Once again there are choices to be made.

You can turn left into Brienner Strasse and go along to the Platz der Opfer des Nationalsozialismus (Square of the Victims of National Socialism), the area of the former Fuhrer and the Nazi party buildings. Then go past the obelisk covered in granite tiles to the Konigsplatz, which became the National Socialist Party's Square. On the northern side is the old **Glyptothek** (Greek and Roman sculptures, open Tues, Wed and Fri-Sun 10am-4.30pm,

Thurs noon-8.30pm), on the western side is a reproduction of the **Propylaon** on the Acropolis in Athens, and on the right hand side is **Lenbach House**. Once the home of the 19th century portrait artist, Franz von Lenbach, the house is now a gallery exhibiting a selection of his paintings as well as a fine collection of 19th century Munich landscape painters. It also has a good cafe and restaurant, and is open Tues-Sun 10am-6pm. At the end of Brienner Strasse is Stiglmaier Platz with the Lowenbrau Keller and beer garden.

OR, you can go straight ahead along Ludwigsstrasse, which has the national library and St Ludwig's church on the right and the university on the left.

At Geschwister Scholl Platz, turn into Leopold Strasse and continue on to the Siegestor (victory arch), where the residential area of Schwabing begins. Near here is the Cafe Stephanie where the great names of literature, e.g. Thomas Mann and Erich Muhsam, met for a bite and where the postcard painter, Adolf Hitler began his career.

OR, if you turn right at Odeonsplatz and go across the **Hofgarten**, you will pass the art gallery that was built during the Third Reich and is an example of the architecture of that era. Continue past there and you will come to the very long and narrow **Englischer Garten**, which has a lake, a Greek temple, a Chinese pagoda, restaurants and cafes, and lots and lots of grass. To the left is **Schwabing**, the traditional students' quarter, but things are becoming a bit expensive there for them.

There are plenty of other interesting sights, but one that stands out is to the west of the city and that is **Schloss Nymphenburg**, the Baroque summer palace of the Bavarian royal family. It can be reached by U-Bahn to Rotkreuzplatz and then tram 12, and it is open Tues-Sun 9am-12.30pm, 1.30-5pm April-Sept, 10am-12.30pm, 1.30-4pm Oct-March. There are guided tours, especially to Ludwig I's Gallery of Beautiful Women, and beautiful pavilions in the grounds.

Another place that may be of interest to some is **Dachau**. It can be reached by train, and has been preserved in memory of those people who were treated so inhumanely and who died there.

Holland

The Kingdom of the Netherlands (Holland) is a constitutional monarchy with a parliamentary system and is one of the most densely populated countries in Europe. The 15,010,500 people live in 40,844 sq km.

Once famous for dykes, windmills, wooden clogs and tulips, it is now probably as well known for its legalisation of soft drugs and its condonation of euthanasia.

The Netherlands is a very flat country, with more than one-fifth of its land under sea level. The language of the people is Dutch. Most people in the towns and cities can speak English.

Climate

The continental influence ensures that there are seasonal extremes of temperature, with the coldest month being January, and the hottest July. The absence of mountains allows the winds from the west to pass straight over the country, bringing some damp weather but not excessive rain.

April and early May is the best time to visit to see the tulips in full bloom.

Entry Regulations

Visitors must have a valid passport, but visas are not required for visits up to three months. It is necessary to check with the Embassy or Consulate in your home country about the duty free allowances current at the time of your visit. There is no restriction on the import or export of currency.

Currency

The currency of the land is the Guilder (Gulden), alternatively known as the Florin, and always abbreviated as Fl or F. It is divided into 100 cents. Approximate exchange rates, which should be used as a guide only, are:

A$	= F1.15
Can$	= F1.20
NZ$	= F1.30
S$	= F1.20
UK£	= F2.50
US$	= F1.55

Notes are in denominations of 1000, 100, 50, 25, 10 and 5 Guilders, and coins are 2 1/2 and 1 Guilder, 25, 10 and 5 cents.

Banks and Post Offices are normally open Mon-Fri 9am-5pm, although some larger post offices also open on Saturday morning.

Most shops are open Mon-Fri 9am-6pm, Sat 9am-5pm. Late night shopping until 9pm is either Thurs or Fri depending on the city. Credit cards are widely accepted in the cities.

Telephone

International direct dialling is available and the International code is 89, the Country code 31. It is expensive to make overseas calls from hotels.

Driving

The Netherlands has a well-maintained road system, and the speed limits are 50kmh in built-up areas and 100kmh on the open road. Driving is on the right, overtaking on the left, and traffic from the right has right of way.

Miscellaneous

Local time is GMT + 1 (Central European Time), and clocks are put forward one hour in summer.

Electricity supply is 220v AC with round 2-pin plugs.

Health - The Netherlands has a very good health system but it is **very expensive for visitors** who are not citizens of the European Community (EC).

Amsterdam

Amsterdam is situated on the River Amstel, and is named after the dam that was built across the mouth of the river in the 13th century. Two series of canals form islands on which the city centre is built, but it appears that the canals actually run down the middle of tree-lined avenues. It creates a very pretty picture, unless you happen to be in the "red light" district, where the windows of the houses are showcases for young ladies displaying their "wares".

History

The Dutch have always had to wage war, not against would-be conquerors, but against the relentless sea whose levels rose to invade the land. Then they had to contend with trying to stop mighty rivers from flooding rich farmland.

For about a thousand years after Roman rule, they seemed to be fighting a losing battle as the sea level rose, piercing the dune belt and forming the Zuider Zee.

In the Middle Ages the tide began to turn. The sea level began to fall slightly, and the windmill was introduced. With these breaks the northern Dutch could relax a little and turn their attention to international trading. The end result was increased prosperity and the rising importance of Amsterdam.

At this stage, The Netherlands was ruled by Spain, but the wealthy merchants rebelled against the feudal system and the interference of the Church. In 1555, the Revolt of The Netherlands broke out against Philip II, and was successful in the northern provinces. Amsterdam continued to flourish while Antwerp, still ruled by Spain, declined. It was not until 1648 that Spain acknowledged the independence of the Dutch.

The modern kingdom began when William I of Orange-Nassau was crowned in 1815. It was in 1848, during the reign of his son, William II, that the Dutch peacefully gained a democratic constitution. The present monarch is Queen Beatrix.

Amsterdam

South Holland: Near the Ulist River

Ireland: Blessington Lakes

Tourist Information

Tourist information offices in Holland are known as VVV (pronounced "Fay-Fay-Fay"), a contraction of Vereniging Voor Vreemdelingsverkeer. They can provide information on all local attractions, public transport, and can arrange accommodation. The main VVV office in Amsterdam is in Stationsplein, in front of Centraal Station, (020) 26 64 44.

In major towns you can also look out for the sign "i-Nederland".

Local Transport

Amsterdam has an efficient local transport system, made up of trams, buses, trains and the Metro. For information on all city transport, ph (020) 627 2727.

Accommodation

Renaissance is a deluxe hotel in the downtown area. Facilities include restaurant, bar, coffee shop, disco, health club, shops and beauty salon.
The Hilton is a superior first class hotel in the midtown area. Facilities include restaurant, bar, shops and beauty salon.
Victoria is a first class hotel in the downtown area. Facilities include restaurant, bar, health club, swimming pool, shops and beauty salon.
Amsterdam has two youth hostels:
Vondelpark, Zandpad 5, ph (20) 683 1744, fax (20) 616 6591.
Stadsdoelen, Kloveniersburgwal 97, ph (20) 624 6832, fax (20) 639 1035.

Food and Drink

Dutch food is normally of a very high standard, and restaurant prices are not quite as high as in other European countries.

Many restaurants are members of the "tourist menu" plan - a three course set menu, organised individually by each place, for a reasonable price. Look for a blue sign outside the cafe.

Another chain of restaurants that is worth trying is **Neerlands Dis.** Members of this display a sign with a red, white and blue soup tureen, and they serve traditional Dutch cuisine.
Dutch soup is in a world of its own, and is highly recommended.

A sign with the word "Pannekoekhuis" outside an establishment means that they specialise in pancakes, both sweet and savoury, and these are usually a meal in themselves and are delicious.

There are many Chinese and Indonesian restaurants in Amsterdam, but surely they are only for the locals. Though, Indonesia having been a colony of the Netherlands, has certainly had a culinary influence.

Shopping

The shopping streets, many of them pedestrian traffic only, begin at Dom Square. One of the busiest is Nieuwendijk. Anything you wish to buy, from cheap, tacky souvenirs to works of art can be found in this area.

Sightseeing

A good place to begin a walking tour of Amsterdam is at the Central Station.

Walk straight ahead along the Damrak to **Dam Square**, where there are always plenty of people standing around the War Memorial in the centre. Some are obviously waiting for other people to meet them, others look as if they are trying to work out where they are, and are possibly the result of Holland's relaxed drug laws. It all looks very peaceful, but beware of pickpockets.

On one side of the Dam is the **Royal Palace**, which was built in the 17th century as a town hall. It is open to the public during Easter, and the summer and autumn school holidays, Mon-Sat 12.30-4pm.

Nearby is the **Nieuwe Kerk** (church) which has been the venue for coronations since 1815, and further on are the tear-drop shaped towers of the **Old Post Office**.

From the Dam take Kalverstraat, a pedestrian shopping street, and at no. 92 there is a narrow alley leading to a beautiful 16th century arched gateway with the city coat of arms. This is the entry to the **Amsterdam Historical Museum**, which is open daily 11am-5pm, and has a very good restaurant. Almost opposite the restaurant is the Schuttersgalerij (Shooters' Gallery), with large paintings of 17th century crack shots, and that leads

AMSTERDAM

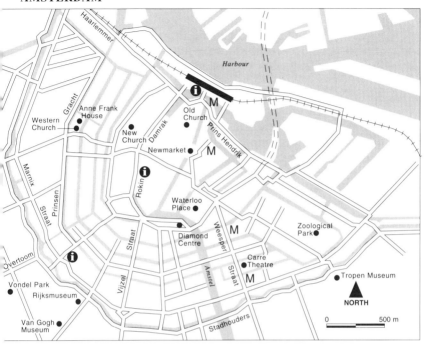

to a beautiful, secluded area with gardens surrounded by 14th and 15th century houses that have been restored and are occupied. For hundreds of years from 1346 this was a home for Lay Sisters, called the Begijnhof. There is a 17th century Presbyterian church at the far end, a tiny Roman Catholic church, and the oldest surviving house in Amsterdam, built of wood and dating back to 1475.

An exit from the Begijnhof leads to a street simply called Spui, then take Kalverstraat to **Madame Tussaud's** where the main attraction is Rembrandt's studio (open daily 9am-6pm). Continue down Kalverstraat to Muntplain, then take Vijzelstraat, or catch bus 49, to Stadhouderkade then turn right (or stay on the bus) and continue on to the famous **Rijksmuseum**, which is open Tues-Sat 10am-5pm, Sun 1-5pm. A world renowned gallery, maybe not equal to the Prado in

Madrid or the Louvre in Paris, but nevertheless not to be missed. As would be expected there is a very good collection of the works of Rembrandt, including the famous *The Night Watch*, but there is much more to see and it is advisable to pick up a guide to the gallery and allow yourself plenty of time.

From the rear of the Rijksmuseum, walk along Museumstraat, turn right into Honthorststraat, then left into Paulus Potterstraat and at no. 7 is the **Rijksmuseum Van Gogh**. This gallery not only has an outstanding collection of Van Gogh's paintings and drawings, it also has his personal collection of works by contemporary artists. It is open Tues-Sat 10am-5pm, Sun and public holidays 1-5pm, and again you should allow plenty of time to study and appreciate the collection.

In the same street, at no. 13, is the **Stedelijk** (Municipal Museum), which is open daily 11am-5pm, and has mostly modern art. Nearby is the **Concertgebouw**, well-known by music lovers. From the concert hall the return trip to the station can be made by tram or bus, or by boat along the canal.

Other attractions do not fit so easily into a walking tour, but the use of public transport will make them easily accessible.

Anne Frank's House, Prinsengracht 263, is to the west of Dam Square. The building is maintained by the Anne Frank Foundation and is open Mon-Sat 9am-5pm, Sun 10am-5pm. For those of us who are old enough to have read the book and seen the movie, this is a very moving museum, those who are younger should visit to learn and remember.

The **Rembrandt Museum** is to the south-east of Dam Square, on Jodenbreestraat near Waterlooplein. The artist lived here for a period and there is a collection of his original etchings. Open Mon-Sat 10am-5pm, Sun 1-5pm.

A few streets away, in J.D. Meyeplain, is the **Jewish Historical Museum** housed in a restored 17th century synagogue.

The international airport is at Schipol, about 16km from the city centre, and just south of that is the town of **Aalsmeer,** the centre of the flower-growing industry. This is where the famous flower auctions take place daily 7.30-11am, and visitors are welcome.

There are two things left to organise, and Amsterdam is famous for both.
❑ The first thing is a trip on the **canals**. These can be organised through any VVV or information centre.

❑ The second is a visit to a **diamond cutting centre**, many of which have tours (although none of them give away free samples). Here are a few:
Amsterdam Diamond Centre, Rokin 1 - open daily except Thurs 10am-5.30pm, Thurs 10am-6pm, 7-8.30pm.
Coster Diamonds, Paulus Potterstraat 2-4 - open daily 9am-5pm.
A. van Moppes and Zoon (Diamond Centre), Albert Cuypstraat 2-6 - open daily 9am-5pm.

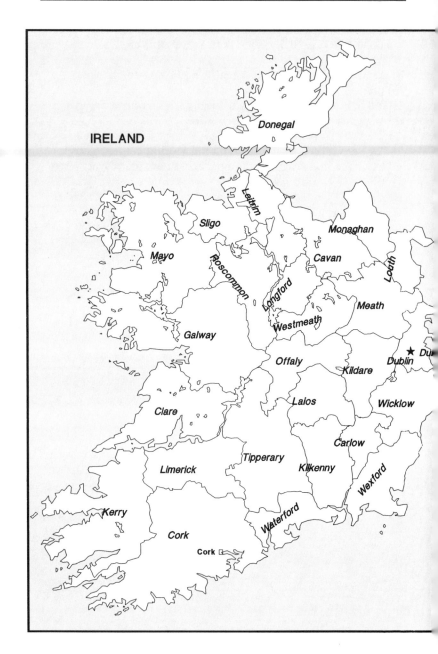

IRELAND

Donegal

Leitrim

Sligo

Monaghan

Mayo

Cavan

Roscommon

Louth

Longford

Meath

Westmeath

Galway

Offaly

Dublin ★ Du

Kildare

Laios

Wicklow

Clare

Carlow

Tipperary

Kilkenny

Limerick

Wexford

Kerry

Waterford

Cork

Cork ⌂

Republic of Ireland

The lush, green island is off the west coast of Britain and has an area of 68,893 sq km with a population of four million. It is joined to Northern Ireland and occupies five-sixths of the entire land mass. Its Irish name is Eire but in 1949 it changed its name to The Republic of Ireland. It became a member of the EEC in 1973. The capital is Dublin. The official language is English and Irish(Gaeilge). English is the mainly spoken.

Ireland is an agricultural country with beautiful scenery. It is noted for the breeding of fine thoroughbred horses.

Climate

Ireland has a moderate climate where the mild south-westerly winds prevail. The Gulf Stream keeps the waters warm. January and February are the coldest months and July and August the warmest. Average temperatures are 39F (4C) -60F (16C). It is advisable to pack a warm jumper and raincoat.

Entry Regulations

A valid passport is necessary. For an extended stay, contact your nearest Irish Embassy.

Duty free allowance is 200 cigarettes or 100 cigarillos or 50 cigars. 1 litre of alcohol over 22% or 2 litres of alcohol not exceeding 22% 2 litres of still wine, 50gm perfume 0.25 litres toilet water. Goods to the value of IR£34. A maximum of 25 litres of beer may be imported as part of the above allowance. Travellers under 15, IR£17. Those under 17 may not import alcohol or cigarettes. No vaccinations are required.

Currency

The currency is the Irish Punt (IR£) divided into 100 pence.

Approximate exchange rates, which should be used as a guide only, are:

A$	= IR£0.45
Can$	= IR£0.44
S$	= IR£0.44
UK£1	= IR£1
US$	= IR£0.62

Notes are in denominations of 50, 20, 10 and 5 Punts, and coins are 1 Punt and 50, 20, 10, 5, 2 and 1 Pence. The best rate of exchange is given by Irish banks. Irish currency should be changed back before leaving the country.

Banks open Monday-Friday 10am-12.30pm and 1.30pm-3pm. **Most Dublin banks are open until 5pm on Thursdays.**

VAT of 15% is added to all goods and services. Cashback is a company which undertakes to refund VAT. Not all stores participate in the scheme. You must have your dockets stamped by customs at your last exit port from the EEC and return the vouchers to Cashback. A fee is charged for this service.

Credit cards are accepted in major stores and hotels.

Telephone

There are public telephones all over the country. International direct dialling is available and the International code is 00, the country code is 353.

Driving

Driving is on the left hand side of the road.
The speed limits are:
30mph in built up areas;
60mph on single roads,
70mph on highways.
Third party insurance compulsory.

Miscellaneous

Local Time is Summer Central European Time.

Electricity is 220v AC. As plugs vary it is necessary to purchase an adaptor and a small transformer.

Health insurance is essential. Take any medication with you and a copy of your prescriptions.

Tipping. A 15% service charge is added to hotel and restaurant bills. No tip is required. Taxi drivers expect 10% and 50p per bag for porters.

Dublin

Dublin is compact by international standards, with a population of the 900,000. It has wide streets, well designed squares and flower beds down the centre of major roads. Main street O'Connell, has most of the banks, shops and theatres. Dublin is situated on the River Liffey which flows into Dublin Bay.

History

Dublin was mentioned by Ptolemy, a geographer, as a place of note in 140AD. The name "Dublin" comes from the gaelic "Dubhlinn" meaning Black Pool, a more modern title than the Irish name in current use "Baile Atha Cliath", the "Town of the Hurdle Ford". The ancient ford was at the site of the present Father Mathew Bridge.

St Patrick visited Dublin in 448 and converted many of the residents to Christianity, and both the settlement and the religion thrived over the next four hundred years. His feast day is celebrated on the 17th March not only in Ireland but in also in many countries (Australia, New Zealand, U.S.A., Canada) to which the Irish have migrated either by force or free will.

In 840 a fortress was set up by some Norse sailors as a base, then in 852 a Danish force took possession of the town. Battles between the Irish and the Danish continued until 1014, when the Danes were finally beaten at the Battle of Clontarf.

The English appeared on the scene in 1170, and Strongbow, Earl of Pembroke took control of Dublin. On a visit to view his new acquisition in 1171, Henry II granted Dublin its first charter.

The Irish were never happy with English rule, and the following centuries saw wars between the two, culminating in the Rising of 1916, which took place over the Easter week.

The Irish Free State was established in 1922, but the Civil War that followed saw Dublin once again in the centre of the action.

Trinity College dates back to 1592. The Georgian squares were built in the 18th century. It has become a cultural centre and a large manufacturing industry has developed. Whiskey distilling, brewing, clothing, glass and food processing are its main industries.

Tourist Information

The Irish Tourist Board has developed a computerised information and reservation system called Gulliver. It has stored all major queries including theatres, sport, concerts, places to visit and transport. Gulliver is in all Irish Tourist Information Offices. The main tourist office in Dublin is at 14 Upper O'Connell Street, ph (01) 747 733, fax (01) 743 660.

Local Transport

Buses are plentiful and reasonably priced with a flat fare. Cruising taxis are not abundant. The best place to find one is at an hotel or bus station.

Accommodation

Deluxe

Hotel Conrad Dublin, Earlsfort Terrace 2, ph (1) 676-5555, fax (1) 676-5424 - 191 rooms with private bath. Central, opposite National Concert Hall. Restaurant, bars, pub, parking. Single £138-£145, double £164-£170.

First Class

The Mont Clare, 74 Marrion Square 2, ph (1) 661-6799, fax (1) 661-5663 - 74 Rooms with private bath. Near sightseeing and station. Restaurants, pub, bar. Single £85-£105, double £105-125 European plan.

Superior Tourist

Georgian House, 20/21 Lower Baggot Street 2, ph (1) 661-8832, fax (1) 661-8834 - 34 rooms with private facilities. 50 yards from St Stephans Green. Licensed seafood restaurant, bar. Single

£32-£35, double £49-£59/72.

Food and Drink

Irish seafood is especially good. Oysters carry the tang of the sea. Brown bread made the way your Grandma made it is the pride of the Irish. Helpings are large.

There is a tourist menu easily recognised by the picture of a chef on the menu cover. These meals are a set price for a three-course meal of simple but good food.

A good selection of wines is available everywhere but it is Guinness and Irish whiskey which are so popular.

The Irish pub is an integral part of Irish lifestyle. It is a gathering place for locals and visitors. Business deals are finalised, family matters discussed, romances conducted and visitors entertained with native wit and song. Every pub has its own charm and clientele. You do not have to drink alcohol to enjoy the lively atmosphere. Many serve coffee and tea and a pub lunch is an economical way to stem the pangs of hunger.

Medieval Banquets are another form of entertainment. Enjoy a wonderful meal and be entertained by musicians, singers and story-tellers. Banquets can be booked prior to departure.

Sightseeing

The city centre has sign-posted walking tours.

A booklet giving maps and background information is available at the information centre. Fans of James Joyce and his *Ulysses* should make sure they obtain a map that details the positions of the relevant plaques throughout the city.

Take a stroll through **Phoenix Park** which covers 1,760 acres. Within the park stands **Aras an Uachtarain**, the official home of the President. At the entrance to the park is Dublin Zoo founded in 1830.

The **Bank of Ireland** building, in College Green, was constructed between 1729 and 1739 to house the Irish Parliament prior to 1800. The British Government sold the building to the bank in 1802. The show-piece of the building is Pearce's House of Lords with its magnificent Dublin glass chandelier dated 1788. There is also an original masterpiece, the House of Commons Mace.

Trinity College is on the east side of College Green and was built in 1592 on the site of a priory that had been taken over by Henry VIII. The university was supposed to further the Reformation in Ireland. The reason for a visit is the Library which has the **Book of Kells** an illustrated manuscript of the gospels from around the 8th century. The work is beautifully done, and although the book is under glass, it is worth seeing.

The **Custom House** on the north bank of the River Liffey is a magnificent building and with the Four Courts is a jewel of Dublin architecture. It was commenced in 1781 and completed in 1791. It was burnt down in 1921 but has been reconstructed.

Dublin Castle was the centre of English power. The official residence of the Lords Deputy and Lords Lieutenant, the seat of State Councils and sometimes Parliament and the Law Courts. Between 1680-1780 wholesale reconstruction gave us the essence of the form we have today.

The State apartments are approached from the main entrance by the Grand Staircase. A lobby to the left of the landing leads to St Patrick's Hall. Since 1938 it has been the place of inauguration of the President of Ireland. **City Hall**, adjoining the castle, was erected as the Royal Exchange between 1769-1799. It is a square building in the Corinthian style with three fronts of Portland stone. **Christ Church Cathedral**, the Church of Ireland Cathedral, was first built in 1038, and the crypt, containing the grave of Strongbow, survives today. A large part of the church is Gothic Revival. **St Patrick's Cathedral** occupies the site of a pre-Norman parish church. It also belongs to the Chruch of Ireland. As such there is no Catholic cathedral in Dublin. It contains some interesting monuments, among them the grave of Jonathan Swift, Dean of St Patrick's Cathedral 1713-1745. He was the author of *Gulliver's Travels*.

The General Post Office is in O'Connell Street, Dublin's main thoroughfare. It was the headquarters of the Irish Volunteers during the 1916 Rising, and it was here that the Republic was announced. There is a series of monuments in the centre of O'Connell Street including the O'Connell Monument, the Parnell Monument and the statue of Father Theobald Mathew.

Opposite Cathedral Street is the Anna Livia Millennium Fountain, which the locals call "The Floozie in the Jacuzzi" because that is exactly what it looks like. Anna Livia represents the River Liffey.

Dublin is noted for its theatres. The *Abbey Theatre* is committed to presenting the works of Irish playwrights. The original building was burnt down in 1951 and a new theatre opened its doors in 1965.

Guinness Brewery is where Ireland's legendary drink is made and it is open to visitors. Enter by the Hop Store, Crane Street. The **Irish Whiskey Corner**. The Irish invented whiskey. Monks of the 6th and 7th centuries learned the distillation process that had been used in Asia for perfume. They turned it into what they considered a better use! They called it Uisce Beatha, Gaelic for "The Waters of Life". The first licence was granted to Bushills Distillery in 1608 and they are still turning it out. Visitors are welcome but you must phone 353-1-725 566 for an appointment.

The **Dublin Literary Pub Crawl** is a three hour entertainment by two actors performing the works of Dublin's famous writers in authentic settings. It starts at Bailey's and continues on to about ten different pubs. Bookings at any local tourist office.

Dublin has many museums, art galleries and libraries all worth seeing if you can spare the time. The **Dublin Experience** is a multi-media show which traces the history of the city from its earliest times and introduces the visitor to the modern city and its people. The soundtrack includes narration by several voices and the background music has been specially chosen. For those in a hurry, this is your answer.

Cork

Cork, Irish name Corceigh, is the second largest city in Ireland with a population of 250,000. It is well inland and lies along the banks of the River Lee which in turn flows into natural harbours. The wide main streets contrast with the narrow alleys of the old part of town.

History

Cork is one of the earliest communities in Ireland. It grew up around a 6th century monastery. The Vikings established the town of Cork as a trading centre in the 900s. An Irish family by the name of McCarthy ruled over the kingdom of Desmond, the region now known as the counties of Cork and Kerry. After the Anglo-Norman invasion, much of the territory was granted to the Fitzgerald family. As Earls of Desmond, they became increasingly Irish.

Cork city remained a centre of English power. In the late 1500s there was an attempted settlement by English colonists. The most famous person to receive land was Sir Walter Raleigh. The Irish attacked the English but lost the battle of Kinsdale in 1601. During the 1600s, Richard Boyle, Earl of Cork became extremely powerful.

Cork became and still is a seat of learning. Among writers from Cork are Frank O'Connor, Sean O'Faolain and Somerville and Ross. Famous people who lived there for some time are Edmund Spenser and philosopher George Berkeley.

Today it exports bacon, dairy produce and livestock. It also has a car assembly, brewery and distillery.

Tourist Information

The Tourist information office is at Tourist House, Grand Parade, Cork, ph (21) 271 081, fax (21) 271 863.

Local Transport

Buses are plentiful but walking is the best way to see this city.

Accommodation

First Class

Fitzpatrick Silver Springs, Tivoli, ph (21) 507 533, fax (21) 507 641 - 100 rooms. Less than 2km from train, 10 minutes from city centre. In spacious grounds. 2 restaurants, bars, gym, squash. Overlooking the River Lee. Single £70-£76, double £80.50-£94.30.

Moderate First Class

Metrapole, MacCurtain Street 2, ph (21) 508 122, fax (21) 506 450 - 91 rooms most with private facilities. Victorian hotel with new wing added. Very central. Restaurant, bar, parking. Single £58-£62, double £70-£85.

Imperial, 14 Pembroke Street, South Mall, ph (21) 274 040 - 101 rooms with bath. Historical old world hotel that has been renovated. 3km from car ferry, 230m from train. Dining room, bar, 24 hr room service. Closed Christmas-New Year. Single £62-£75, double £100-£110.

Many of the pubs in the town and the country have comfortable rooms with breakfast and high tea for a reasonable rate.

Food and Drink

There are plenty of restaurants serving seafood.
Try trout, prawns or salmon. There are excellent steaks, lamb and stews. Don't forget the whiskey and Guinness.

Shopping

There are outstanding bargains in light tweeds, fine linen, lace, scarfs, knitwear, shirts, porcelain and Waterford crystal.

Sightseeing

A trail guide book is available from the information office.
University College was built in 1845 and is part of the National University of Ireland.

   St Ann's Shandon Church is famous for its bells. Cork also has Cathedrals, including St Finbar's. It is the riverside with its strips of parkland which make Cork so attractive. Rest on one of the seats and enjoy the sunset.

Sights Further Afield

The most popular excursion is only five miles from Cork. It is a visit to Blarney Castle. Climb to the top and attempt to kiss the **Blarney stone.** The stone is under the battlements and it requires both agility and nerve to attempt this feat. There is nothing between the stone and the ground 26m below. The successful kisser is supposed to be endowed with considerable eloquence. The view from the top of the castle is well worth while.

   The city of **Waterford** in the southeast is where you can see the famous Waterford Crystal being produced, and maybe buy a special souvenir of Ireland.

Map of Italy

Rome: St. Peter's

Rome: Trevi Fountain

Rome: Piazza de Popolo

Italy

The Republic of Italy encompasses the Apennine Peninsula, Sicily, Sardinia, and to the north, the Alps. The population is around 57,000,000 and the area of the country is 302,225 sq km.

The numerous art and architectural treasures, as well as the mediterranean climate along the coast and in the south, make Italy one of the oldest holiday lands of Europe. There is more industry and it is more densely populated in the north, and where the west coast of the peninsula has harbours, the east coast only has flat beaches. The Mezzogiorno area in the south is the least developed and the most disadvantaged.

Italian is the language of most of the country, with French spoken in some of the alpine districts, and German in parts of the Trentino. English is widely spoken in the tourist centres.

Climate

Summer can be very hot, oppressively so, in Rome and places to the south. The capital averages 18-31C in July and 4-12C in January, whereas Milan in the north averages 18-29C in July and -2-+4C in January.

Entry Regulations

Visitors must have a valid passport, but visas are not required for a stay of three months or less.

The duty free allowance is 400 cigarettes or 100 cigars or 500 grams of tobacco, 1 litre of alcoholic beverages if alcoholic content is in excess of 22%, 2 litres if alcoholic content is less than 22%. The import of foreign currency is unlimited.

No vaccinations are required for any international traveller.

Currency

The currency of the land is the Lira (plural lire). Approximate exchange rates, which should be used as a guide only, are:

A$	= L1200
Can$	= L1150
NZ$	= L1050
S$	= L1150
UK£	= L2600
US$	= L1620

Notes are in denominations of 100,000, 50,000, 20,000, 10,000, 5,000, 1,000 and 500, and coins are 200, 100, 50, 10 and 5.

Banks are generally open Mon-Fri 8.30am-1.20pm, and for one hour in the afternoon, usually between 3pm and 6pm, but this can change from bank to bank, so it is best to check the hours of the bank closest to where you are staying before you are desperately short of money. **Exchange counters are found at main railway stations and airports. It is best to exchange money as soon as you arrive in the airport as it is always a hassle trying to change money in the city.**

Post Offices in the main cities are open Mon-Fri 8.30am-6.30pm, Sat 8.30am-12.30pm, and those in smaller towns are open Mon-Fri 8.30am-1.30pm, Sat 8.30am-12.30pm. They can also be closed! Remember you are in Italy.

Shopping hours are generally 8.30am-1pm, 3.30-7.30pm.

Credit cards are widely accepted in shops and restaurants, but not in petrol stations.

Telephone

International direct dialling is available and the international code is 00, the country code 39.

Driving

Italians have the reputation of being amongst the worst drivers in the world, something that does not altogether displease them. Though everyone seems to know what they are doing and the traffic flows. Courtesy to other drivers can seem conspicuous by its absence. The best advice for travellers from overseas is to try and stay out of other people's way.

The speed limits are not apparently widely known, but are:

Cars of up to 1100cc -	built up area -	110 kph
	open road -	130 kph
Vehicles over 1100cc -	built up area -	130 kph
	open road -	130 kph.

Seat belts are compulsory in the front seat. The locals seem very blasé which seems to be often ignored.

It is possible to hire a car with a driver's licence issued in your home country, but hiring a car is an expensive option. Not only are the rates higher than in most other countries, but there are 25 motorway companies ready to extract toll from drivers, and the toll depends on distance travelled.

Note: If you decide to drive, never leave anything in a parked car as it is almost guaranteed it will not be there when you return. Keep everything out of sight- in the boot at the very least.

Miscellaneous

Standard time is GMT + 1, with daylight saving in operation from the end of March to the end of September.

Electricity is 220 volts with round plug pins.

Health - it is absolutely necessary to have adequate medical insurance to guard against a stay in an Italian general hospital.

Siesta is a fact of life in Italy, and you have to learn to live with it. From about 1.30pm to around 3.30pm nothing happens. Everyone goes home, has lunch, and presumably a siesta.

Rome

Rome, "The Eternal City", sits on the banks of the River Tiber and is the capital of modern Italy. To some it is "the finest city in the world" but to others its great historical sites, and even St Peter's, do not make up for the dreariness of the place, nor for the fact that a visitor never feels completely safe. When in Rome, do what the Romans do if that makes you happy, but leave all your valuables and your passport in the hotel safe while you're doing it.

History

The origins of Rome go back to around 600BC, and the people who lived there were not Italians but Romans, made up of Latin and Sabine stock. Originally ruled by kings, Rome became a republic in 509BC and was quickly a force to be reckoned with. Using whatever means necessary, ie war or diplomacy, its provinces soon included all the countries of the Mediterranean including parts of Africa.

The republic lasted 400 years, then Julius Caesar, the great conqueror, tried to take over as a dictator and was assassinated in 44BC. His adopted son, however, fulfilled his ambitions and ruled as Emperor Augustus Caesar from 30BC to AD14, a period of great peace and prosperity.

Then came Christianity. Its original followers were persecuted, fed to lions, crucified, and generally made to feel unwelcome, especially by the Emperor Nero. But when Constantine became the Emperor he declared Christianity to be the official religion of the Empire.

It has been discovered that during the 2nd century AD, there were more than a million people living in and around Rome, some of them in high-rise apartments - it was truly the capital of the world.

When the capital moved to Constantinople, the Popes became the virtual rulers of Rome. Unfortunately, some of the Popes were not what you could really call "holy men", and in fact they became progressively worse, hitting rock bottom in the eleventh century. In the 14th century they moved to Avignon, and Rome deteriorated to a town of around 20,000.

The Renaissance and the return of the Popes to the city saw the birth of the Rome of today. Popes Julius II and Leo X were great patrons of the arts and caused many great buildings to be erected, beginning with the Palazzo Venezia, and St. Peter's.

Tourist Information

The **main information office** is near the Stazione Termini at 5 Via Parigi, ph 488 9200, and there is another inside the station opposite platform 3, ph 487 1270.

There is also an office in the customs area of the Fiumicino (Leonardo da Vinci) airport.

McDonalds, believe it or not, are in the middle of town near the *Spanish Steps* at the top of the *Corso.* You can use their toilets for free (you have to pay everywhere else - including in Stazione Termini, the main train station) and they have an excellent free tourist map of Rome with suggested tours.

Local Transport

Metro

Rome has an underground system. Linea A and Linea B intersect at Termini. It is an efficient system but you must have a ticket. These can be purchased from kiosks with the name *Tabacci* (tobacconists) which sell newspapers, etc. You can use this to get about anywhere, eg to *Ottaviani* then walk to St Peter's etc . There is also a tram and bus service which operates throughout the city. Most of the things that visitors want to see can be reached on foot.

Taxis

The official taxis are yellow and these are the only ones to get. Make sure the driver turns the meter on otherwise you will have an unpleasant scene at the end of your trip as you haggle over money. The locals always win.

Transport from the Airport

When you arrive at *Fumicino* and make your way to the general area after passing through customs avoid men soliciting rides to the city. They normally come up to you saying 'taxi'. A train now operates from Fumicino to Ostensi (L12,000) once every 20 minutes and also another goes to Termini (L15,000). A taxi can cost as much as L100,000.

> **If you are have to get an early flight from the city to Fumicino which is a good 30 km from the city organise a transfer from your hotel before you leave home. The alternative is to ask the hotel when you are there to organise your taxi so the price is controlled. Normally about L60,000.**

You have to face the fact that in Rome you are going to end up paying more than you ought whether it is in the café, the taxi or shop. No matter how experienced a traveller you are, the end result will be the same. If the locals don't get you, the gypsies will try. Beware grubby children bearing carnations.

Accommodation

Holiday Inn Crowne Plaza Minerva, 69 Piazza della Minerva, ph (6) 474 3551, fax (6) 474 7307, is the newest hotel in the city centre.

Borocco Hotel, 4 Via della Purificazione, ph (6) 487 2001, is a 4-star hotel that a quite reasonable.

Gregoriana, 18 Via Gregoriana, ph (6) 679 4269, fax (6) 678 4258, is a former convent near the Spanish Steps. A 3-star hotel and good value.

Rome's youth hostel is *Foro Italico* - AF Pessina, viale delle Olimpiadi 61, ph (6) 323 6267, ph (6) 324 2613.

There are a lot of 2 star hotels around Termini and especially near Piazza del Republica. Prices vary but Termini is not a nice place to hang around at night.

As it is the eternal city there are quite a few places run by religious orders that provide accommodation for visitors. You do not have to be a Roman Catholic to take advantage of these places. The cost is very reasonable, and the lodgings are, of course, safe. You do have to obey the rules though. Ask at the Information Office at the airport. If no luck there or at Termini go to the Vatican and ask at the *information centre* on the left hand side of the square as you face the main entrance.

Food and Drink

A dish on any menu that has the word "Romana" in its name is supposed to have originated in Rome, and lovers of Italian food probably include several of these among their favourites. The specialties of Rome, however, are supposedly tripe, brains and other forms of offal.

One thing visitors do notice is that dishes cooked in the old country tend to have a lot more oil in them than their counterparts in foreign countries.

You won't have to go far to get a cappuccino, but getting a hot one is not so easy. When ordering, try asking for it to be *bollente.*

The oldest restaurant in Rome is the *Campana* at 18 Vicolo della Campana, off Via della Scrofa, ph 656 7820. It has apparently been operating since 1518, but the atmosphere is a bit heavy, and so is the food - closed Monday.

One of the 'in' places to eat is *Ristorante '34*, 34 Via Mario Fiori, ph 679 5091. It specialises in modern Italian cuisine, and has some pretty amazing dishes - closed Monday.

Another 'in' place, especially with the young, is *Trattoria all'Arancio* at 51 Via dell'Arancio, ph 6847 0095.

> An important tip is to eat out at a trattoria, rather than a ristorante which is usually much more expensive; and another is to try the local house wine, which is often surprisingly good, and not the more expensive bottled variety.

Shopping

The fashion shopping district is along *Via dei Condotti* and the streets on either side of it and intersecting it. There are famous labels from France and Switzerland as well as local designers. This is not the place for bargain shopping, but if you appreciate fine material and workmanship, it is worth a visit. *Via Frattina* has shops with probably the most reasonable prices in the area.

Along the *Corso* are the more down to earth outlets, and

amongst the shops you may find a few offering quality leather and silver goods.

Down from *Piazza Barberini* there are some quality men's clothing stores, and between *Piazza del Popolo* and *Piazza de Spagna* there are a lot of boutiques.

Sightseeing

The centre of the city is generally agreed to be **Piazza Venezia**, and it can't be missed because it is home to the **Monument to Victor Emmanuel II**. Locals call the monument "the typewriter", and it does resemble one from the front, but whatever you call it, it really is different. There have been suggestions that it be demolished, but that would probably cost more than it is worth.

The square is named after another of its buildings, **Palazzo Venezia**, built in 1455 by Cardinal Pietro Barbo, who later became Pope Paul II.

Some of the most important Roman streets radiate from Piazza Venezia: **Via IV Novembre,** which leads to the Via Nazionale, then on to Piazza Esedra and the Railway Station; **Via del Plebiscito**, which runs into Corso Vittorio Emmanuele and leads to St Peter's; **Via del Corso,** which leads to Piazza Colonna and Piazza del Popolo; and **Via dei Fori Imperiali,** which passes through the centre of ancient Rome.

Walking Tour of Old Rome

Almost behind the Victor Emmanuel Monument is the **Capitoline Hill**, one of the seven hills on which the city is built, and the **Piazza del Campidoglio** or Capital Square. The square, the buildings surrounding it, and the staircase leading to it, were designed, and the construction was supervised by Michelangelo for Pope Paul III, who wanted to impress Charles V. Of course, Michelangelo was never noted for his speed of execution, and the buildings were not ready in time for Charlie's visit.

On three sides are the **Senator's Palace** (in the centre and now the Town Hall), the **Palazzo dei Conservatori** (on the right) and

From the Piazzo Venezia you can take Trolley Bus 64 to St Peter's and the Vatican.

Arch of Septimus Servus

the **Palazzo dei Musei** (on the left). The last two have incredible collections of ancient works of art and sculpture.

The long staircase to the right of the Capitolien Museum leads to the **Church of St Maria in Aracoeli**, which dates from the 6th century. It has several chapels, and the tombs of several important people with headstones sculpted by artists such as Donatello, but the piece de resistance is the *Bambino d'Aracoeli*, a wooden statue of the Child Jesus, carved out of olive wood from the Garden of Gethsemane. It is kept in the Sacristy Chapel, except during the Christmas season when it forms the centrepiece of the Crib.

The Roman Forum
The **Roman Forum** can be reached by taking the path to the right of the Senator's Palace. The Forum was the cradle of Roman civilisation, and the city's most important social and political site. This is the original Forum, but as Rome grew and developed it became too small, and other Fora, or meeting places, were developed. Consequently there is the Imperial Fora, Trajan's Forum, the Forum of Augustus, the Fora of Caesar, Vespasian and Domitian.

The original Forum suffered considerable damage from invasions over the years, both from armies and from antique collectors. It was totally neglected over the centuries, and was even used at one stage to corral cattle. Excavations began in the 18th century and it didn't take the workmen long to realise what a dilapidated state the Forum had reached.

Unless you are well versed in early Roman history, it is suggested that you either visit the Roman Forum as part of a guided tour, or pick up a book about it at your hotel desk or at any of the numerous souvenir stalls. Without someone or something to explain what the various columns, arches and part-buildings are (or were), the whole thing can look like a demolition site when the workers are at lunch. Actually the books are very good because they have drawings and photographs of reconstructions of the original buildings.

Arch of Titus
At the far end of the Forum is the **Arch of Titus**, built to commemorate the victories in Jerusalem of Vespasian and Titus. This is very interesting because on the inside there are reliefs showing a victory parade through Rome displaying the loot from the Temple including silver trumpets and a menorah (seven-branched candelabrum).

Palatine
To the right a path leads up to the **Palatine**, Rome's oldest hill and the place where Romulus is supposed to have founded the city in 754BC. During the republican period this was "nob hill", home to the noble families, then when Augustus became Emperor he built his palace. Over time other Emperors added to the buildings, then in the Middle Ages it was converted into a fortress, and in the 16th century it became a vast garden. Archaeological excavations in this area have proven that the hill was actually inhabited as early as the Iron Age, and in fact the dig is probably the most important in Rome. Among the ruins of various buildings, to the east of the hill, is the Palatine Stadium, or Racecourse. Historians are not sure whether this 160m x 80m was used as one or the other, or perhaps both, and they also have not been able to ascertain whether it was open for public as well as private functions.

Make your way beyond the stadium to the Belvedere Terrace, where you can get a great view of the **Circus Maximus**. The Terrace was built by Septimus Severus (193-211).

Circus Maximus
The Circus Maximus was built by Tarquinis Priscus, and added onto by Julius Caesar. It was thought to have held as many as 100,000 spectators. It was to here, rather than to the Colosseum, that the Romans flocked to see the persecution of the Christians ordered by Emperors Nero, Domitian, Trajan, Septimius Severus, Decius, Valerian and Diocletian. To the last-named is attributed the "Great Persecution".

Arch of Constantine
Return to the Arch of Titus and walk to Via di San Gregorio,

ROME

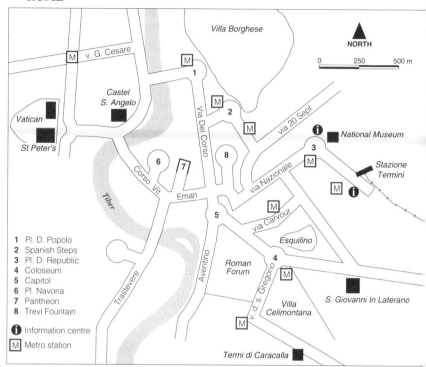

Villa Borghese

NORTH

0   250   500 m

v. G. Cesare

Castel
S. Angelo

Vatican

St Peter's

Via Del Corso

via 20 Sept

National Museum

Stazione
Termini

Corso Vit.

Eman

via Nazionale

via Cavour

Tiber

Esquilino

Trastevere

Aventino

Roman
Forum

v. d. S. Gregorio

Villa
Celimontana

S. Giovanni In Laterano

Termi di Caracalla

1   Pl. D. Popolo
2   Spanish Steps
3   Pl. D. Republic
4   Coloseum
5   Capitol
6   Pl. Navona
7   Pantheon
8   Trevi Fountain

ⓘ   Information centre
Ⓜ   Metro station

turn left and stop at the **Arch of Constantine**. Built to commemorate the Emperor's victory at the bridge of Milvio in 312, the arch is the best-preserved in Rome. The reliefs on the arch facing you feature some of the battles of Constantine. The rest relate to the exploits of other Emperors, Trajan, Hadrian and Marcus Aurelius, and have been taken from other monuments. Near the arch is a cone-shaped fountain, the **Meta Sudans,** where gladiators washed themselves after leaving the Colosseum.

Colosseum

Next stop is the **Colosseum,** or the Amphitheatrum Flavium as it was known in its heyday. Construction began in 72AD under Emperor Vespasian on the site of a stagnant lake. It was dedicated by Titus in 80AD at a celebration that lasted more than three months and saw the killing of 500 wild animals and more than a few gladiators. It was an incredible structure with:

underground passages and tunnels from which people and animals could be brought into the arena; facilities for transforming the arena into a lake to stage naval battles; and devices for covering the whole stadium with a large awning in the case of bad weather. Considering the ravages of time including an earthquake in the 5th century, what is standing today is impressive, but try to imagine the whole of the building covered in marble, with a marble statue of a god or VIP in each of the arches on the second and third floors. Pretty amazing!

Via dei Fori Imperiali to the Piazza Venezia
The Via dei Fori Imperiali leads from the Colosseum back to the Piazza Venezia, passing some interesting ruins and buildings on its way. First is the **Temple of Venus and Rome**, built by Emperor Hadrian in 135AD, then the **Church of Santa Francesca Romana**, which was first built in the 10th century, but has been restored so often that none of the original buildings have survived. Inside, however, there are some pieces dating from the 12th and 13th century, including the original Campanile, and the tomb of Pope Gregory XI. The church is part of a monastery that houses the Museum of the Forum.

Next is the one remaining nave of the **Basilica of Maxentius**, completed by Constantine in 312AD, with vaults reaching to 25m high and a fine coffered ceiling. The Basilica had two entrances, one onto the Via Sacra, the other towards the Colosseum. Today it is used for concerts in the summer.

The **Church of Saints Cosma and Damian** is visited next. It was founded by Pope Felix IV in 527AD on the site of the Templum Sacrae Urbis, and was restored in the 17th century. There are some very interesting 6th century mosaics in the apse.

Imperial Forums
Now we come to what are known as the **Fori Imperiali** (Imperial Forums). They were built in the last days of the Republic to accommodate the larger population. The first was built by Julius Caesar, followed by Augustus, Vespasian, Domitian, Trajan and Hadrian. During the Middle Ages this important area became buried under tons of soil, and it was not until 1924 that excavations began.

The **Forum of Nerva** has only a few columns left, which are known as the "colonnacce" and have a fine frieze.

The **Forum of Augustus** is entered from the Piazza del Grillo, to the left of the Via dei Fori Imperiali. It commemorated the Battle of Philippi when Augustus defeated Brutus and Cassius, the murderers of Caesar. This was the beginning of Augustus's climb to fame. The forum was built on the site of the Temple of Mars Ultor, and some remains of this can be seen.

The **Basilica Argentaria**, from the later years of the Empire, is near here and was used for commercial meetings.

The **Forum of Caesar** is to the right of the Via dei Fori Imperiali, and was built in 54BC to commemorate the Battle of Pharsalus. The Temple of Venus Genetrix once stood here and three of its columns still remain. The statue of Julius Caesar is a copy. The original is in the Campidoglio.

The **Forum of Trajan** is below street-level. It was built to celebrate victories over the Dacians. Designed by Apollodorous of Damascus, it consisted of a piazza, two libraries, temples, basilicas and monuments, and the Basilica Ulpia. The most outstanding feature now is **Trajan's Column**, which stands 42m high. It has a series of reliefs depicting the victories of the Emperor in the 1st century AD, and his vault is under the column. The statue on the top, however, is St Peter, placed there by order of Pope Sixtus V in the 17th century.

   Trajan's Market was a group of buildings next to Trajan's Forum where merchants and markets operated. The Palace of the Knights of Rhodes from the 15th century is now on the site.

The Vatican State

It is one of the smallest in the world, and it is the spiritual centre of the Roman Catholic religion. The Vatican became independent of Italy in 1929, but its history began with the Emperor Constantine, who wanted the first great Christian church to be built on the spot where St Peter was martyred.

St Peter's Basilica

The present St Peter's was commenced in 1506 on the site of Constantine's church. The original architect was Bramante, but his plan was modified in 1547 by Michelangelo, whose apse and dome now remain. Maderno took over and changed the ground plan from a Greek cross to a Latin cross. Then, in 1657, Bernini completed the building with the Colonnade of St Peter's Square and its statues of 140 saints.

The obelisk in the centre of the square was brought from Egypt by Caligula to stand in the nearby Nero's Circus, where many Christians including maybe St Peter met their maker. The cross on top was not, of course, part of the original obelisk.

St Peter's is the second largest church in the world. The facade is 114.69m long and 45.44m high, and approached by a grand stairway with statues of St Peter and St Paul at the sides. The balustrade is supported by eight Corinthian columns and has enormous statues of Christ and John the Baptist in the centre, and the apostles, except St Peter, at the sides. There are nine balconies, and it is from the centre one that the Pope bestows his benediction. Five open entrances lead into the vestibule, which is 71m long, 13.5m wide and 20m high. Opposite the main door of the basilica, over the central entrance, is the mosaic of the Navicella (St Peter walking on the sea) which was originally in the old Basilica of Constantine. To the left is a statue of Charlemagne; and to the right one of Constantine. There are five entrances to the church. The last door on the right, the Porta Santa, only being opened every 25 years for the Jubilee.

The interior of the church has an area of 16,160 sq km and is 211.5m long, the central arm is 186.36m long, 27.5m wide, 46m high; the transept is 137.5m long, and the cupola from the lantern measures 132.5m. There are 229 marble, 533 travertine, 16 bronze, and 90 stucco columns and 44 altars.

There is no doubt about the fact that the place is huge, and there are even marks on the floor showing where other churches would fit, eg St Paul's in London. But, many people remark on the fact that it does not seem to have an air of, for want of a better word, "holiness" as other churches do. Maybe it is just too big. As you are wandering around looking at the altars, canopies, etc, etc, make sure you do not miss out on Michelangelo's *Pieta* in the first chapel to the right of the entrance. Sculpted when he was only twenty-five years old, and now behind bullet-proof glass because some crazy actually attacked it, the *Pieta* is one of the very few sculptures that he actually signed - on the Virgin's sash - and many think it to be the best work he ever did.

Positioned on the pillars along the central nave are statues of the founders of institutions within the Catholic Church who have been canonised. **A bronze statue of St Peter** on the left hand side near the main copula of St Peter is venerated by thousands of pilgrims. You will note his right foot has worn away from constant touching.

The statues in the four colossal piers supporting the copula are St Andrew (apostle), St Helena (Mother of Emperor Constantine), St Veronica (wiped Christ's face during the carrying of the Cross) and St Longinus (Roman soldier who pierced the crucified Christ's side with a lance and became a Christian martyr). In the centre, the baldercino designed by Bernini towers above the main altar where only the Pope says Holy Mass. **Beneath this is the tomb of St Peter.** The tomb is in part of the left pillar which houses an ornate box containing the palliums which are bestowed on Archbishops by the Pope. From above, on the main floor of the nave, many Catholic pilgrims renew their commitments to their faith with what is called the *Creed*, said privately.

On the left-hand side, back almost opposite the *Pieta*, is an altar

> **In recent years on the right hand side as you face the main altar and some metres on past the *Pieta* is a chapel with the Blessed Sacrament exposed. Vatican personel are stationed here and permit people to go in who wish to pray. 'Tourists' are not permitted. There is another more open chapel on the left closer to the main altar and away from the hubbub of the central nave.**

dedicated to **St Pope Pius X** who lived this century. A man reputed for his holiness he was canonised soon after his death.

Near the right-hand side pillar of the central nave near the bronze statue of **St Peter** is the entrance to the **floor beneath the main nave.** Here are chapels where various Popes, certainly the most recent, are buried. Below this level are what is called the **Scarvi** which in essence are catacombs. You have to have prebooked to go here. Enquire at the Vatican information office.

The **Vatican Palace** is a large group of buildings, mostly museums, galleries, libraries and archives, but a few house the Pope and the Pontifical Court and are, of course, off-limits to visitors. However, the Pope's office can be seen from the Square from which he prays *the Angelus* at noon on Wednesdays and Sundays with pilgrims.

Vatican Museums

The **Vatican Museums** can be reached by a shuttle bus from the Information Office on the left of the piazza (daily except Wed and Sun), or it involves quite a hike from St Peter's around the Vatican walls by way of Via di Porta Angelica, Via Leone IV and Viale del Vaticano.

It would be impossible to see all the treasures of the museums in one visit, or even a few, so it is best to follow one of the four sign-posted tours which take from ninety minutes to five hours. **The most popular is Tour A, for which you can hire an audio tour. If you are a fan of the work of Raphael, note that the four rooms devoted to his pieces are part of Tour C.**

Sistine Chapel

All the tours lead eventually to the **Sistine Chapel**. Named after Pope Sixtus IV for whom it was built, the Chapel is now used only for Conclaves (meeting of Cardinals to elect a new Pope) and certain solemn ceremonies.

For those who are not really into art the first thing to realise is that Michelangelo did not paint all of the chapel; the six panels on each side wall were the work of others, and they are extremely well executed. The rest, the work of Michelangelo, is simply breathtaking.

The chapel paintings have recently been restored and there is

> **The museums are open daily 9am-2pm (at Easter and July-September 9am-4pm), except that it is closed on all religious holidays - Jan 1, Feb 11, May 1, June 29, Aug 15, Nov 1, Dec 8, Dec 25.**
> **There is an admission charge.**

a great deal of controversy about the end result. Some claim that the top layer of Michelangelo's works has been removed, leaving much brighter colours than he envisaged, but the Vatican is quite content with the restoration saying that the colours on show now are exactly what the artist had intended. Let us hope the Vatican is correct; it would be a catastrophe if any of the work was ruined in any way.

The restoration was financed by a Japanese company in return for exclusive rights to all pictures. Consequently, it is not permitted to take photographs of any kind in the chapel. This fact does not seem to have got through to Japanese tourists though, who often give the impression of proprietorship.

Back to Rome

One other tour that can be made from Piazza Venezia, is to the Trevi Fountain. Take Via Cesare Battisti to Piazza dei SS Apostoli, which is named after the **Basilica of SS Apostoli**, near the Palazzo Colonna. Built in the 6th century, the church has been restored many times, and once completely rebuilt. It houses some valuable works of art.

Trevi Fountain
The narrow alleyways at the side of the square, then Via San Marcello and Via delle Muratte eventually lead to the famous **Trevi Fountain**, one of the most beautiful fountains in Rome, and indeed in the world. It was built for Pope Clement XII and finished in 1762. The central figure is Neptune in his chariot, drawn by two sea-horses preceded by two tritons (mermen). When I first saw Trevi I was amazed that it was actually attached to a building, the facade of the Palace of the Dukes of Poli. I had the impression from seeing the movie years ago that it was of free-standing construction.

The name Trevi comes from the word "trivio", or crossroads, or exactly where three roads meet. Rather aptly named it must be agreed. There was a bath-house complex on the site as early as 20BC, and the reliefs on the sides of the arch tell the story of soldiers returning from battle and being told of a natural spring by a young girl. The water was called Virgin Water in her honour. The custom of throwing a coin in the water to ensure a return to Rome seems to have no established beginning. It used to be that one had to drink the fountain's water, but maybe it was a bit murky at times. The Fountain was restored a few years ago, and it really is a sight to behold.

From here you can walk to *Piazza Barberini* and along Via Barberini, where there are some really good boutiques for men and women, as well as a few travel agents. Or, you can walk the other way to Via Del Corso, probably the main street of Rome. It runs in a straight line from Piazza Venezia to the Piazza del Popolo, becoming Via Flaminia and continues to the Milvio Bridge. There are palaces on both sides of the street, and in the Middle Ages it was the scene of the famous Berber horse races of the Carnival.

Catacombs

No trip to Rome would be complete without a visit to a catacomb, and we suggest the **Catacombs of Priscilla** at Via Salaria 430. Take Trolley Bus 35 from Stazione Termini, get out at Piazza Crati and walk a short distance. Ring the bell at the convent door and a Benedictine nun will be only too happy to guide you through the catacombs. Two attractions not to miss are: the oldest known painting of the *Virgin and Child with Isaiah*, from the 2nd century and found in a small chapel. And a fresco depicting the earliest known *The Breaking of the Bread at the Last Supper*. The catacombs are open Tues-Sun 8.30am-noon, 2.30-5pm, Admission charge.

Other Churches

Rome is littered with Churches, both ancient and more recent, each with a history. From St John Lateran Basilica - the church of Rome, to St Mary Major near Termini with its magnificient ceiling leafed with gold from the 'new world', a gift of Phillip II of Spain. Before coming to Rome determine what your priorities are and stick to them.

Information for some travellers - Gesu Church of St Ignatius of Loyola - Piazza de Gesu, ph 678 6341; St Paul outside the Walls, Porta San Paolo (via Linea B), ph 541 0341; Our Lady of Peace, tomb of Blessed Josemaria Escriva, founder of Opus Dei, viale Bruno Buozzi 73, Parioli district, ph. 808-961.

Florence

Florence lies in the heartland of Tuscany, on the banks of the River Arno. To say that it is a beautiful city, is not doing it justice, it is simply like no other.

History

Florence was originally a Roman camp, and has been the seat of a bishop since the 4th century.

In the 13th century Florence was probably the richest city in Europe. Her currency, the florin, was international tender. Her people were, in the main, moneylenders and cloth and woollen merchants. There was no shortage of gold and rich families, but the richest of all were the Medici and they became the ruling dynasty. Fortunately for Florence the Medici were patrons of the arts, in fact the greatest patrons in Europe. They almost single-handedly financed the Renaissance. Cosimo the Elder was the patron of Donatello and during his time the first Renaissance buildings appeared in the city.

His grandson, Lorenzo the Magnificent, was a good friend of Botticelli, and took Michelangelo into his home as a 15-year-old and treated him as a son.

Other great masters who spent at least some, if not all, of their lives in Florence include: Giotto, Brunelleschi, Masaccio, Botticelli, Leonardo da Vinci, Raphael and Vasari.

Tourist Information

The Tourist Information Office is at 1R Via Cavour, ph 276 0382, next to the Palazzo Medici.

FLORENCE

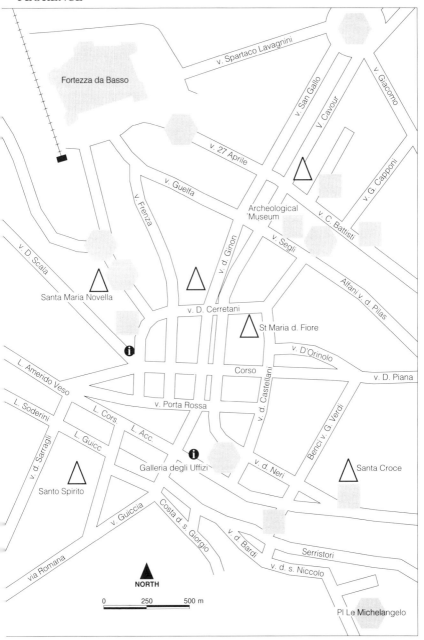

Fortezza da Basso

v. Spartaco Lavagnini

v. San Gallo

V. Cavour

v. Giacomo

v. 27 Aprile

v. Guelfa

v. Frenza

Archeological Museum

v. G. Capponi

v. C. Battisti

v. D. Scala

v. d. Ginon

v. Segli

Alfani v. d. Pilas

Santa Maria Novella

v. D. Cerretani

St Maria d. Fiore

v. D'Orinolo

L. Amerido Veso

Corso

v. D. Piana

L. Soderini

L. Cors.

L. Acc.

v. Porta Rossa

v. d. Castellani

Benci v. G. Verdi

v. d. Sarragli

L. Guicc.

Galleria degli Uffizi

v. d. Neri

Santa Croce

Santo Spirito

v. Guiccia

Costa d. s. Giorgio

v. d. Bardi

Serristori

via Romana

v. d. s. Niccolo

NORTH

0   250   500 m

Pl Le Michelangelo

Local Transport

There is a bus service, but you can walk to everything that is worth seeing.

Accommodation

Excelsior is the top of the range in Florence. It is situated on the Arno at 3 Piazza Ognissanti, ph 264 201, fax 210 278.

Berchielli, 14 Lungarno Acciaiuoli, ph (55) 264 061, fax (55) 218 636, and *Lungarno*, 14 Borgo San Jacopo, ph (55) 264 211, fax (55) 268 437, are also on the banks of the river, but are 4-star and consequently more reasonable, although lacking some of the facilities of the Excelsior.

Florence's youth hostel is *Villa Camerata*, Viale Augusto Righi 2-4, ph (55) 601 451, fax (55) 610 300.

Food and Drink

Although there are a large number of restaurants in Florence, it is really a place where you only eat if you are hungry. That is not to say that the food is not good, it is just that there is nothing special about it.

If you want to try a typical Florentine eatery, one where the locals go, then head for *Il Latini*, 6R Via Palchetti, ph 210 916. It is near the Piazza Goldoni, and is open Wed-Sun for lunch and Tues-Sun for dinner.

If you in Florence on a Monday when Il Latini is closed, the most similar place would be *Sostanza*, 25 Porcellana, ph 212 691, near Ognissanti. It is open for lunch Mon-Sat and dinner Mon-Fri.

Shopping

There is no doubt that the quality of goods bought in Florence is first class, but you have to pay for it. Gone are the days when you could pick up a leather bargain, but even so window shopping is a delight because of what is on offer.

There are more shoes for sale in Florence than in any other city in Italy, and a walk down the Via dei Tornabuoni will have dedicated shoppers drooling. This street is the continuation of the bridge next to the Ponte Vecchio when heading away from the Uffizi.

There are a couple of quite good markets that sell fake 'designer' gear with fake 'authentic' labels, and some of it is worth a close look. Enquire at the information centre.

Sightseeing

A walking tour can start at those two symbols of Florence - the **River Arno** and the **Ponte Vecchio**, the quaint old bridge that crosses it. Originally the little shops on the bridge were owned by butchers, but the Medici replaced them with jewellery shops and they are still there.

Walk down Via Por Santa Maria to the **Piazzo della Signoria**, a slightly odd-shaped square, and the **Palazzo Vecchio**, which was built in the 14th century for the city's Priors. It is now the Town Hall, and can be visited to see the Hall of the Five Hundred and the Hall of Justice. Incidentally, the copy of Michelangelo's David in this square is where the real one originally stood before it was taken under cover to help preserve it. The **Loggia dei Lanzi** is in front of the Palazzo. It was built in the late 14th century for public government ceremonies, but it is now an open-air museum containing some famous sculptures such as Cellini's *Perseus,*

Next stop is **Galleria degli Uffizi**, more commonly known as 'The Uffizi', one of the great galleries of the world, and the biggest in Italy. It has forty-five rooms containing what can only be described as art 'treasures'. Over a million people visit the Uffizi each year, and often it is necessary to join a long queue to gain admission, but it is well worth it. The ground floor has the restored Church of San Pier Scheraggio with its frescoes, Andrea del Castagno's *Famous Men* and Botticelli's *Annunciation.* The first floor has the prints and drawings section, but only the room

> **Museums are normally open Tues-Sat 9am-1pm (or 2pm), 3pm (or 4pm)-7pm, Sun 9am-1pm. Smaller museums may, however, vary their hours. Entry fees are quite high for some of the galleries, though not when you consider what you will be seeing, but be prepared. All persons over the age of 60 years are admitted free to all national museums and galleries on production of their passport.**

at the top of the stairs on the left is open to the general public. The second floor has the major collection, and has three corridors of mainly sculpture surrounded by rooms containing the paintings. The ceiling in the third corridor should not be overlooked. The rooms with the paintings are set out two ways: chronologically for the Florentine; and geographically for the rest. Each room is numbered for easy identification.

It is necessary to backtrack now to get to the **Cathedral** complex. The church is one of the longest in the world. Longer are the Cathedral on the Ivory Coast, St Peter's in Rome and St Paul's in London. Most churches exude an air of holiness, this one doesn't. The most famous thing about it is Brunelleschi's dome, an architectural masterpiece. It consists of two domes with a space between (that can be climbed by anybody fit enough) that give the appearance of a cupola without any supports. It took Brunelleschi over fifteen years to complete the dome, and it has recently been discovered that he is buried in the cathedral, probably as a reward for his labours.

The cathedral has another famous attraction, the East Gate of the **Baptistry**. Here are found the ten panels by Lorenzo Ghiberti that are known as the *Doors of Paradise*. They begin with Adam and Eve in the top left and continue horizontally. Experts have stated that the sculpture is "a painting in bronze", and it really is quite breath-taking. It is very difficult to take a photo of the doors because there is also someone closely examining them. (Unfortunately, some of the panels will probably be replaced by copies when you are there. The originals are being restored in what is turning out to be a lengthy job.)

The **Museo dell' Opera del Duomo** is a museum containing the works of art that were once in the cathedral, and it is at 9 Piazza del Duomo. It has some interesting exhibits such as Donatello's choir loft, the gear that Brunelleschi used for the dome, and a *Pieta* that Michelangelo smashed because it wasn't good enough and someone reassembled 300 years later.

From the left side of the cathedral walk up Via Ricasoli to no. 60 and you have found the **Galleria dell' Accademia**, the home of Michelangelo's *David*. It would be worth the price of admission if that was the only work on display, but not so. There are also Michelangelo's unfinished *Captives* that he worked on for the tomb of Pope Julius II; and paintings by such artists as Fra Filippo and Ghirlandaio. It is a nice, bright and airy gallery.

A block or so behind, and forming one side of the Piazza Santissima Annunziata, is the **Ospedale degli Innocenti** (Gallery of the Hospital of the Innocents). Originally an orphanage, it is now a gallery, that has some fine Renaissance paintings, including Ghirlandaio's *Adoration of the Magi*.

The Piazza San Marco, off Via Cavour, almost opposite the Galleria dell' Accademia, has the Dominican monastery of San Marco, where Fra Angelico lived and painted. It has now become a gallery dedicated solely to his work. His paintings are not as worldly as the others of the Renaissance, but his genius cannot be denied.

Back almost where we began, east of the Palazzo Vecchio, is the old **Santa Croce**, the biggest Franciscan church in Italy. The first thing you see when you walk in is the absolutely awful tomb of Michelangelo, the work of Vasari. Others buried here include Machiavelli and Galileo. Worth looking at now are Giotto's *The Death of St Francis* and other frescoes by his pupil Taddeo Gaddi. In the cloisters is the portico of the Pazzi Chapel, which some say is the greatest achievement of Brunelleschi.

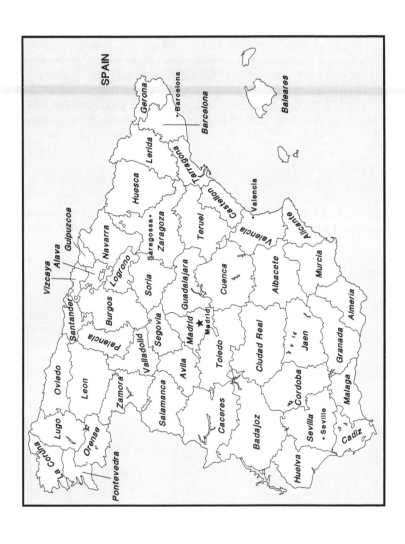

Spain

Spain is a constitutional monarchy, with a total area of 504,782 sq km of which the mainland takes up 492,463 sq km. It has a total coastline of 3144 km. The population is 39,433,942, and the main cities are Madrid, Barcelona, Valencia, Seville, Malaga and Saragossa. The official language is Castilian (otherwise known as Spanish), which is derived from Latin but includes many Arabic words. Catalan is spoken in the north-east and is more like Provencal. The Basques, who come from the Bay of Biscay area, have a completely different language of unknown origin. As a visitor the majority of people you come into contact with will be able to speak some English

Climate

Even in summer the north coast is frequently rainy and misty. The central plateau has extremes of temperature from -12C in winter to 35C in summer, and the wettest months are March and April. The provinces on the Mediterranean have high humidity in summer, while Andalusia has no real winter except in the very high places.

Entry Regulations

Visitors must have a valid passport, and Australians must have a visa for visits up to 30 days.

People from the UK, the US and New Zealand do not require visas, and other nationalities should enquire at the Spanish Consulate in their home city.

The duty free allowance is 400 cigarettes or 100 cigars or 500 gm of tobacco; 1 litre of alcoholic beverage (over 22 degree strength) or 2 litres of alcoholic beverages (under 22 degree strength) or 2 litres of wine; 500 gm of perfume.

No vaccinations are required for any international traveller.

Currency

The currency of the land is the Peseta (Ptas). which is divided into 100 centimos. Approximate exchange rates, which should be used as a guide only, are:

A$	= 93ptas
Can$	= 90 ptas
NZ$	= 80ptas
S$	= 90 ptas
UK£	= 200ptas
US$	= 125ptas

Notes are in denominations of 10,000, 5000, 2000 and 1000 Pesetas, and coins are 500, 200, 100, 50, 25, 10, 5 and 1 Pesetas.

Banks are open Mon-Fri 8.30am-2pm, although some big city banks remain open until 4.30pm and also open on Sat 8.30am-1pm. Outside banking hours money changing facilities will be found at airports, train stations and booths near the main tourist areas.

Post offices are open Mon-Fri 9am-2pm, although again the Head Post Office in each city normally remains open until 8pm.

Shops are normally open Mon-Sat 9am-1pm, 4.30-8pm. Supermarkets are usually closed on Sat afternoon. On fiesta days, which are plentiful, it is possible that all shops and services will cease to operate, but not in the main cities.

Credit cards are widely accepted, and there are plenty of ATMs in the large cities.

Telephone

International direct dialling is available and the International code is 07, the country code 34.

Driving

An International Driving Licence is necessary to hire a car, but in practice an overseas licence is often accepted.

'A' roads are toll motorways with a speed limit of 120kmh; 'N' roads are main roads with a speed limit of 90kmh; and 'C'

roads are local roads where nobody is in a hurry. Traffic drives
on the right.

Miscellaneous
Local time is GMT + 1, with daylight saving in force from the
beginning of April to the end of September.

Electricity is 220 volt AC, 50 cycles, with round two-pin plugs.

Health - Good health facilities are available, but it is advisable to
have health insurance.
Milk should be boiled, and water away from the city areas
should be avoided. Bottled water is available.

Madrid

Madrid, the capital and largest city of Spain, is situated in the
geographical centre of the country at 700m above sea level,
making it the highest capital in Europe.
    It is a pretty city with wide streets and spacious, green parks.

History
Spain came under Roman rule in 206BC as a result of the Punic
wars between Carthage and Rome. When the Western Empire
collapsed, Madrid, Toledo, Segovia, Soria and Guadalajara were
taken over by the Visigoths, a Germanic people, who took the
language and religion of their captives. This kingdom was
overthrown by the Arabs in 711, although a small band of nobles
held out for 300 years.
    The 10th century saw the Christians of the north-west begin a
revival that, over the next three hundred years, reduced the size
of the Moslem holdings. Then in 1212, the Moors were defeated
by Alfonso VIII, and came away with Granada as the only area
over which they had any influence. This too came to an end, but
not until 1492.
        Christian Spain was made up of several independent
kingdoms, but the wedding of Isabella of Castile and Ferdinand
of Aragon in 1479 united the two main royal houses and formed

the basis of the modern country.

In 1522, the Hapsburg Charles I of Spain, who was also the Holy Roman Emperor, granted Madrid the title of "Imperial and Crowned City", after the unsuccessful Revolt of the Comuneros. In 1651, Philip II made Madrid the capital of the great Spanish colonial empire.

Tourist Information

Information offices are found at:

Princesa 1, Edificio Torre de Madrid, ph 241 2325;
Barajas Airport, ph 205 8656;
Charmartin Station: Vestibulo, Puerta 14, ph 315 9976.

Local Transport

The best form of transport is the Metro, which is fairly cheap and goes to all the important parts of town. There are ten lines that are marked on a handy pocket map that is obtainable from the information office or at a Metro station.

The thick red lines of the city bus routes are almost impossible to work out unless you are a native of the city, but the yellow lines showing the minibus routes are much easier to see and to follow.

Taxis are everywhere and can be hailed in the street, but as usual they are an expensive option.

Accommodation

Embajada is a first class hotel in the downtown area. Facilities include restaurant, coffee shop and health club.

Gran Hotel Colon is a first class hotel in the midtown area. Facilities include restaurant, bar, coffee shop, health club, swimming pool and beauty salon.

Parque Avenidas is a first class hotel in the downtown area. Facilities include restaurant, bar, coffee shop, health club and swimming pool.

Madrid has two youth hostels:

Marcenado, Calle Sta Cruz de Marcenado 20, ph (91) 547 4532.
Richard Schirrman, Casa de Campo, ph (91) 463 5699.

Food and Drink

Madrid is famous for its cafes and bars (*tabernas* and *tascas*) and there are many around the Cortes, the Puerta del Sol, the Plaza Mayor and the Plaza de Santa Ana.

Drinks are usually served with *tapas*, which may consist of olives, sausage, oysters, shrimps, or a type of calamari.

Spain produces many fine wines, and available everywhere is that nectar of the gods, *sangria*, a concoction made from red wine, brandy, mineral water, orange and lemon juice, and heaps of sugar, and served with fruit and ice cubes - don't miss it.

The cuisines of every Spanish province are available in Madrid, but its own specialties are *cocido*, a soup/stew made from chick peas, meats and vegetables, and *callos* a highly-seasoned tripe dish. Of course, all the traditional Spanish dishes are available, such as *gazpacho* and *paella*.

Meals are usually eaten quite late in Spain. Lunch is between 1.30 and 2.30pm and dinner between 8.30 and 9pm. Keep an eye out for the fixed-price tourist menu, which must consist of three courses plus bread and wine.

Shopping

The busiest shopping area is along Calle de Preciados, between Puerta del Sol and the Plaza de Callao, much of which is a pedestrian mall. The large department stores are here, including *Celso Garcia, Cortefiel, El Corte Ingles* and *Galerias Preciados*.

For upmarket and expensive boutiques, it is hard to go past Calle de Serrano, between Calle Diego de Leon and the Plaza de la Independencia. Calle Goya, between the Plaza de Colon and Calle del Conde de Penalver is another popular area with its share of department stores, and leather outlets.

Do not expect the staff in department stores to be able to speak English. Unless you make an effort to speak Spanish don't expect them to go out of their way to help you. Young people would be best to head for Calle de la Princesa, near the University City.

Sightseeing

The centre of the city is **Puerta del Sol**, where all the main roads converge, and where the main Metro station is found. The name means "Gate of the Sun", as it was once one of the main entrances to the town, and it has witnessed some important historic occasions. On May 2, 1808 the Spanish resistance to Napoleon began here; in 1835 the Liberals took possession of the Post Office building; in 1912 Canalejas, the then Prime Minister, was assassinated by anarchists; and in 1931, from the balcony of the Old Post Office, the Second Republic was proclaimed.

The Old Post Office, now the police headquarters, was built in the 18th century and its construction caused the demolition of two whole blocks of houses. The building is of granite, white limestone and red brick, and has two arcaded inner courtyards. The clock tower was a later addition, and so was the iron cage that contains the gilded ball that announces the beginning of the New Year to the enormous crowds that gather in the square.

The cafes and bookshops for which Puerta del Sol was famous have disappeared, but there are still many specialty shops, confectioners and people that make it one of the liveliest places in Madrid.

From Puerta del Sol, walk about 400m north along Calle del Preciados or Calle Montera to the **Gran Via**, which runs from the Calle de Alcala to the Plaza de Espana. A street of office blocks, banks, department stores, cafes, cinemas, Metro stations and underground parking stations and Bingo halls, the Gran Via is the centre of modern and commercial life.

The **Plaza de Espana** is a green expanse where old meets new: the old quarters of the Hapsburg and Bourbon regimes meet the Gran Via of the 1930s and the high rise of the 1950s. The square is dominated by the monument in its centre. It is dedicated to Cervantes who is seated looking down on statues of his characters Don Quixote and Sancho Panza, who in turn are looking out over a lake. It is a very attractive edifice, and the park is very popular with workers at lunch-time, and with people going to or coming from the many nearby cinemas.

The **Palacio Real** (Royal Palace) is in Calle de Bailen, a short walk from the Plaza Espana, although the main facade is on the south side, facing the Plaza de la Armeria.
The palace is open Mon-Sat 10am-1.30pm, 4-6.15pm and Sun 10am-1.30pm (summer); Mon-Sat 10am-12.45pm, 3.30-5.15pm

Switzerland: Zurich's Bahnhofstrasse

Lucerne: Chapel Bridge and Water Tower

and Sun 10am-1.30pm (winter) and conducted tours are available in English, French, German and Spanish.

Worth seeing are the apartments occupied by Charles III,the throne room and the incomparable tapestry collection.

From Plaza de Espana Metro station it is possible to catch a train to **Casa de Campo**, a 1700ha park that houses a swimming pool, an amusement park, a cableway, and the **Parque Zoologico** (Zoo). Previously a royal hunting ground closed to the public, the park is now visited by an average of 50,000 cars and 500,000 people every week. The zoo is open daily 2-7pm.

If you are not interested in visiting the zoo, from Calle de Bailen take Calle Mayor to the **Plaza Mayor**, which has been an important part of the city since the 17th century. Not only was it the commercial centre, but it was also the site of royal proclamations, canonizations, and a few executions, as well as bullfights and dramatic plays. The statue of Philip III in the middle of the square now presides over the Christmas fair, and the many people who congregate in the pavement cafes, or at the stamp market.

The Plaza Mayor is a pedestrian area, and has two exits on each side leading to the Calle de Toledo, Calle Mayor and Calle Postas. Near the Casa de la Carniceria there are steep steps leading down to the **Cava de San Miguel** quarter, a fascinating part of old Madrid with plenty of restaurants, cafes and tascas.

From Plaza Mayor exit onto Calle Mayor, continue to Carrera de San Jeronimo then to Plaza Canovas del Castillo and from there you will see the **Museo del Prado** on Paseo del Prado.

King Charles III wanted to urbanise the Spanish capital, and part of his dream was a new plan for the Prado de San Jeronimo, or St Jerome's Meadow. The meadow consisted of the gardens of the former San Jeronimo monastery, and the gardens of the Buen Retiro Palace, which was a popular picnic spot for the locals at that time. The outstanding figure in Spanish architecture at that time was the Neo-Classical Juan de Villaneuva (1739-1811), so he was given the brief and designed the Botanical Gardens, the Astronomical Observatory, and in 1785, the present Prado.

The building was not opened until 1819, during the reign of Ferdinand VII, and was called the Museum of the Royal Picture

Collection. That was the beginning of one of the greatest art collections in the world, housed in one of the greatest galleries. If anyone is visiting Madrid for one day, they should forget the rest and head for the Prado. True lovers of art who are in Madrid for five days could happily spend their whole time in the Prado. There is not room here to describe the whole collection, and to choose one section would not do justice to the rest, so the only advice given here is not to miss visiting. It is open Mon-Sat 9am-7pm, Sun and public holidays 9am-2pm, and there is a cafe and a bookshop.

Barcelona

Barcelona is the capital of Catalonia, one of the 17 semi-autonomous regions of Spain. Catalonia consists of four provinces, is home to around 15% of Spain's total population, and covers 6% of the country's area. The provinces are Lleida, Girona, Tarragona and Barcelona, and their inhabitants have their own language, Catalan.

Barcelona city has a population of around four million people, and was the site of the 1992 Summer Olympics.

History

Very early in time, Barcelona's shores was visited by Phoenician and Greek traders, and historians believe that the Carthaginians established a settlement called Barcino, after their General.

A Roman town dates from the 2nd century BC, and excavations under the Museu d'Historia de la Ciutat and the Placa del Rei have brought ruins of that town to light.

Control of the town passed from the Romans to the Visigoths, then the Moors, then the Franks, who in the 870s founded the House of the Counts of Barcelona.

The House of Barcelona ended with the death of Martin I in 1410, and Catalonia became associated with the kingdom of Castile, although retaining its rights and constitutions that limited the king's control.

During the War of the Spanish Succession (1700-1714), Catalonia was against the Bourbon Felipe V, so when he took control he punished Catalonia by revoking its constitution, which was not restored until 1932. It was short-lived though, and was again revoked in 1939. In a referendum in 1979 the people of Catalonia voted in favour of self-government, and autonomy was granted soon after.

In the interim, though, Barcelona flourished. The Universal Exhibition of 1888 saw over two million people visit, and that of 1929 showed a much larger city with the results of the Modernist architects on display.

Tourist Information

There is an information office at the airport that is open Mon-Sat 9.30am-8pm, Sun 9.30am-3pm. There is also one at the Estacio Barcelona Central Sants (railway station) that is open daily 8am-8pm.

There is a government office at Gran Via de les Corts Catalanes 658, ph 301 7443, which is open Mon-Fri 9am-7pm, Sat 9am-2pm, and the city has offices in Placa Sant Jaume and the Palau de la Virreina, La Rambla 99. They are open daily 10am-8pm.

Local Transport

The Metropolitan Transport Corporation produce a booklet called "Guia del Transporte Publico de Barcelona y su Area Metropolitana" which is available at their offices at Sants station; Placa de Catalunya; the Universitat metro station; Ronda Sant Pau 43; and Avinguda Borbo 12. These are open daily 8am-7pm, and can also advise on special deal fares and tickets.

Tickets can also be purchased at metro stations, savings banks and some buses. For information, ph 336 0000.

The very good bus service operates daily from 5.30am-10.30pm, plus a few night services. From June 23 to September 16, the Bus Turistic (no. 100) runs on an "explorer" route. It stops at 15 main attractions and passengers can get on and off at any or all of its stops. The ticket can also be used on the Tramvia Blau (tram), and the funiculars to Tibidabo and Montjuic.

The Metro has four underground lines, 1, 3, 4 and 5, that connect with above and underground train services run by the

Sagrada Familia

Generalitat which extend beyond the city. All stations have maps of the network displayed. The Metro operates Mon-Fri 5am-11pm, Sat-Sun and Holidays 5am-1am.

Accommodation

Rialto is a 3-star hotel situated in the hart of Barcelona's Gothic Quarter and next to the Town Hall.

Regina, is a moderate first class hotel near Catalunya Square and the famous Ramblas Boulevard.

There are four youth hostels in Barcelona:

Mare de Deu de Montserrat, Passeig Mare de Deu del Coll 41-51,

ph (93) 210 5151, fax (93) 210 5151.
Hostal de Joves, Passeig Pujades 29, ph (93) 300 3104.
Pere Tarres, Numancia 149-151, ph (93) 410 2309, fax (93) 419
6268. *Studio,* Duquesa d'Orleans 58, ph (93) 205 0961.

Food and Drink

As with any place that is close to the sea, fish is frequently on the
Barcelona menu with cod being the main one. The favourite
meat is pork, closely followed by lamb. Pasta is widely used, and
replaces rice in many of the traditional dishes, such as paella.

Some of the local specialties are: Espinacs a la Catalana is
spinach with pine nuts and raisins; Arros negre is rice cooked in
squid ink; and pilotas are spongy meat balls flavoured with pine
nuts, cinnamon, parsley and garlic.

Barcelona has eight wine producing areas, so there is quite a
choice of both whites and reds. Generally speaking they are very
good. Drinks are actually less expensive here, not that they cost
less, but the measures are larger.

Agut, Trinidad, 3 (corner Avinyó,8). ph 315 1709 Open Tues-Sat.
The Agut family (3rd generation) make a popular Catalan meat
dish. Popular restaurant. 3,000 ptas average meal. Amex, Diners,
Visa, MC.

Blau Mari, Moll de la Fusta, Plaza de Colon, Ediculo,2, ph 310
1015, seafood dishes, popular during summer, air-conditioned,
4,000ptas average meal. Amex, Diners, MC, Visa.

Casa Chus, Avda Diagonal, 339 ph 207 0215. Well known
restaurant covering all dishes. 4,000 ptas average meal. Amex,
Bisa, Diners, MC.

Giardinetto Notte, La Granada del Penedés, 22, ph 218 7536.
Closed Sundays and all of August. Excellent salmon dishes,
italian and whatever you want. Good place to meet. 3,000 ptas
average meal. Amex, Diners, Visa, MC.

Eldorado Petit, Dolores Monserdá, 51, ph 204 5153. One of the
better restaurants in Barcelona. 7500ptas average meal. Amex,
Diners, Visa, MC.

Shopping

Barcelona is not really a place for shopping. Of course there are
shops, and plenty of them, but everything is so expensive that it

is better to save your money for another place.

Sightseeing

The Harbour is one of the largest and most modern in Spain, and which services commercial and passenger ships.

In the Placa de Portal de la Pau, adjacent to the waterfront, is the **Christopher Columbus Monument**. Built in 1888, the base is decorated with scenes from Columbus' life and voyages, and the whole is topped by an 8m bronze statue of the man himself. A lift, on the harbour side, can take visitors to the top, but the view is not great.

There is also a reproduction of the *Santa Maria*, Columbus' flagship on his voyage of discovery to America in 1492, on the harbour side of the monument. The ship is open daily 9am-2pm, 3pm-dusk.

Also on Placa del Portal de la Pau is the **Maritime Museum** (Museu Maritim), housed in the halls of the old Royal Shipyard.

The shipyard was established in the 13th century, and was declared a national monument in 1976. (There are the remains of some of the old town walls on the south side.) The exhibits are continually being added to and cover all facets of shipping and sailors, from full scale replicas of olden day ships, to models in glass bottles. A visit is recommended and the museum is open Tues-Sat 10am-2pm, 4-7pm; Sun 10am-2pm.

A **Cableway** runs from the slopes of Montjuic, to Torre de Jaime 1, then on to Torre de San Sebastian, a steel pylon on the New Mole. The cablecars run from 11.30am until 8pm daily.

The Passeig de Colom, a wide tree-lined avenue, runs north-east from the Columbus Monument to the Head Post Office, which is close to the Lonja (the Exchange).

The Ramblas

They are a series of main tree-lined streets that run north-west from the Columbus Monument to, and through, the Placa de Catalunya, the biggest square in Barcelona, to the Avinguda de la Diagonal, a wide main street of the new town.

The Ramblas have many pavement cafes and news stands, and attractions include:

Rambla de Santa Monica - Wax Museum open daily 11am-1.30pm, 4.30-7.30pm.

Carrer Nou de la Rambla (west of Rambla dels Caputxins) - Museum of the Theatre (Museu de les Arts de l'Espectacle) housed in a building designed by Antoni Gaudi. It is open Tues-Fri 11am-2pm, 5-8pm.

Carrer de Sant Pau - Sant Pau del Camp (St Paul in the Fields), a Romanesque church built in 1117, outside the town walls.

Rambla de Sant Josep - flower market held every morning. The Mercat (Market Hall) is on the left, with a fish market in the centre. Near the Market is the former Palace of the Vicereine, with two bronze horses guarding the entrance. Built between 1772 and 1777 for the Viceroy of Peru, it was occupied by his widow until 1791, but now it is the home of the Museum of Decorative Art, open Tues-Sat 10am-2pm, 4.30-9pm, Sun 9am-2pm. Also in residence is the Postal Museum.

Placa de Catalunya - the end of the Ramblas, and also the Old Town quarter. The square is very large and has gardens and ponds. Many of the leading banks are found around here. To the east, in Carrer Sant Pere Mes Alt, is the Palace of Catalan Music, another Modernismo building, this time designed by Domenech i Muntaner. Barcelona University is on the Placa de la Universitat, which is reached by following Carrer de Pelai from the south corner of the Placa de Catalunya.

Passeig de Gracia, a very wide street with four rows of plane-trees, runs parallel to the Rambla for just over a kilometre. There are two buildings in the street that were designed by Antoni Gaudi: no. 43 Casa Battlo, which was inspired by the story of St George; and no. 92 Casa Mila, which is a great example of his work but not apparently inspired by anything but the Art Nouveau Movement, which the Spanish called Modernismo. The Casa Mila has guided tours Mon-Fri at 10am, 11am, noon, 1pm, 5pm and 6pm, Sat at 11am noon and 1pm (except in August). For those interested in Antoni Gaudi, there is a museum devoted to him in the Parc Guell, which is in the section on the north of the city.

Also in the Passeig de Gracia, at no. 35, is Casa Lleo-Morera which was completed by Domenech i Montaner in 1905, with a bit of help from the leading artists of the day. The building has been refurbished and on the first floor is the headquarters of the local tourism office called the **Patronat Municipal de Turisme. It** is open Mon-Sat 9am-2.30pm, 3.30-5.30pm.

The Old Town (Gothic Quarter or Barri Gotic) is basically between the Ramblas and Via Layetana, and is the surviving part of the medieval town. It is a collection of narrow streets, mostly pedestrian, with all kinds of shops, bars and restaurants.

The **Town Hall** is on the Placa de Sant Jaum, north-east of the Rambla dels Caputxins. The building dates from the 14th century, but the main part of the front is from 1847. The sides of the building, however, still have some Gothic parts. Inside the building, the Council Chamber is from the 14th century, and the Salon de las Cronicas has murals by Jose Maria Sert.

Opposite is the Palau de la Generalitat, which was built in the 15th century to house the Estates of Catalonia. It now has the offices of the provincial government, and a beautiful inner courtyard in the Gothic style.

The **Cathedral** is situated on Monte Tabor, the highest point of the Old Town, and was built on the site of a Romanesque church which itself had been built on the site of an early Christian basilica. The present Gothic building was started in 1298, but it was not finished until 1448 so most of the building dates from around the 14th century.

Inside the church there is a feeling of great space, and that is typical of the Catalan Gothic style. There are 29 side chapels, one of which has the historic "Christ of Lepanto". It was used as a figurehead on the flagship of Don John of Austria's fleet that defeated the Turks in 1571. Also in this chapel is the tomb of the sainted Bishop Olegarius who died in 1136. In the last chapel on the north there is a black Virgin similar to the famous Virgin of Montserrat. Other features not to be missed are the stained glass, the choir-stalls in the nave, and the pulpit, all from the 15th century, and the 16th century retablo in the Capilla Mayor. Steps from the **Capilla Mayor** lead down to the crypt where there is the chapel of St Eulalia, one of the city's patron saints, to whom the cathedral is dedicated. Her alabaster sarcophagus is the work of an Italian artist in the 14th century.

The **Cloister** is on the western side of the Cathedral. It was built between 1380 and 1451, and is surrounded by numerous chapels dedicated to different saints. At the south-west corner, in the Chapterhouse (Sala Capitular) is the Cathedral Museum, which is open daily 11am-1pm.

South-east of the Cathedral is Placa del Rei, and in that square is the Casa Padellas, a replica of a medieval mansion built in 1931. When excavating for the foundations workmen came across many Roman remains. The Casa Padellas houses part of the **Historical Museum** (Museu d'Historia), the remainder is in the nearby former church of Santa Agata, and in the Salon de Tinell, a large hall that is part of the former royal palace where Colombus met with Ferdinand and Isabella when he returned from his first trip to America. The museum is open Tues-Sat 9am-8.30pm, Sun 9am-2pm.

Take Carrer de la Princesa from the square to Carrer Montcada, then look for no. 15, the Palau Berenguer de Aguilar, a Late Gothic mansion that houses the **Picasso Museum**. Open Tues -Sat 9am-2pm, 4-8.30pm, Sun 9am-2pm. The works are arranged in chronological order and include paintings, drawings, lithographs and etchings from all of the various periods. Not to be missed if you are at all interested in modern art.

Montjuic

It means "Hill of the Jews" is on the south side of the city and was so named because of the large Jewish cemetery that was once on the site. Some of the gravestones are now in the Archaeological Museum in Passeig Santa Madrona, with the Parc de Montjuic.

The northern side of the 213m hill has been progressively developed since the late 19th century, and for the 1929 Universal Exhibition, the 202ha park acquired pavilions, sports facilities and exhibition halls, together with gardens and fountains. Added to these were the Anella Olimpica (Olympic Ring) that was the principal site of the 1992 Olympic Games.

Access from the harbour is by cableway to the Parc de Miramar on the north-east slope. From Avinguda del Parallel, there is a funicular, with the first section underground, that meets up with a cableway that goes up to the castle. The funicular operates noon-2.50pm, 4.30-9.15pm.

The **Castle** (Castell de Montjuic) has a Military Museum in its centre, but its main attractions are the city views obtained from the bastions at its corners. There are also great views from the flat roof of the citadel.

On the northern slopes of the hill is found a **Parc de Atraccions**, or amusement park, with sideshows, a Ferris wheel, a theatre and restaurants. This park is open Mon-Fri 6.15pm-12.15am, Sat to 1.15am, Sun noon-12.15am.

The north-west side of the hill has many pavilions that were built for the 1929 Exhibition and are now used as museums.

North of the City

Carrer de Mallorca runs off Avinguda Diagonal at Plaza Mossen Verdaguer, and its most fascinating building is the **Templo de la Sagrada Familia** (Church of the Holy Family). Experts say it is the principal work of Antoni Gaudi (1825-1926), who unfortunately died before it was completed, without leaving behind a set of plans. He did leave a scale model, but this was badly damaged when anarchists attacked the building in 1935. So it remains unfinished, although Jordi Bonet Armengol, son of one of Gaudi's collaborators, is now the chief architect and he believes that one day the building will be completed. Work moves very slowly.

Some try to describe the church saying that it is Gothic and Neo-Gothic combined with Art Nouveau, but whatever you like to call it, it seems to be a hotchpotch of real and fairy-tale architecture. (Is there any truth in the rumour that the English word "gaudy" derives from the name of this Spanish architect?)

The building is open daily 9am-7pm, and there is an audio-visual presentation on the history of the project near the entrance. There are parts of the building that are open to the public daily 9am-7pm.

If you want to see more of Gaudi's work, head for **Parc Guell**, in the north-west of the city (Metro station Vallcarca - Line 3). The park was designed by Gaudi and worked on between 1900 and 1914. It contains his house, which is now a museum, and many other Gaudi buildings and details for buildings.

Seville

The fourth-largest city in Spain and capital of Andalusia, Seville lies on the left bank of the Rio Guadalquivir at an altitude of 10m. It has a population of around 680,000, and one of the hottest climates in mainland Europe, reaching 48C.

The 1992 International Exhibition was held in Seville, at the same time as the Olympics were in Barcelona.

Andalucians speak Castilian, the 'normal' Spanish.

History

There was already an established town on the site when the Romans arrived in 205BC, but by the time of Caesar it was a very important port called Colonia Julia Romula. During the 5th century AD it was ruled firstly by the Vandals, then by the Visigoths. The 8th century saw the Moors take over, then the Umayyads, the Almoravids and the Almohads from 1147. In the latter half of the 12th century many fine buildings were erected, and the city had a larger population than Cordoba.

In 1248 the town was recaptured by Ferdinand III of Castile, who made it his capital for the remaining four years of his life. After his discovery of the New World, Colombus was given a ceremonial reception in Seville. Voyages by Amerigo Vespucci and Magellan were orchestrated from Seville and it became the world's busiest and most important port.

In 1717 Seville lost its trade monopoly to Cadiz, mainly because the Rio Guadalquivir has a constant problem with silting, and facilities at Cadiz had been drastically improved.

Tourist Information

The city tourist office is located at Costurero de la Reina, Paseo de las Delicias 9, ph 423 44 65; and the provincial tourist office is at Avenida de la Constitucion 21B, ph 422 14 04.

There is also an information desk at San Pablo Airport, ph 425 50 46.

Local Transport

The city's bus service is operated by Tussam and there are route maps at bus stops. A complete map of the network - Plano de Red Lineas - can be picked up at tourist offices. Single journey fares are purchased on board the bus, but Bonobus saver tickets for ten trips are available at tobacconists (estancos).

Horse-drawn carriages operate around the central sightseeing area, and will take up to four people. Always settle on a price before getting into the carriage.

Accommodation

Cuidad de Seville is a first class hotel in the downtown area. Facilities include restaurant, bar, coffee shop, health club, swimming pool, shops and beauty salon.

Gran Lar is a first class hotel in the downtown area. Facilities include restaurant, bar, coffee shop, health club, shops and beauty salon.

Seville's youth hostel is at Isaac Peral 2, ph (95) 461 3150, fax (95) 461 3158.

Food and Drink

A good thing to remember when you are in a Seville restaurant is that *callos a la andaluza* means "tripe stew", which may not titillate your taste buds.

During the 1992 Expo many restaurants realised that it would be a good idea to have menu translations, and that practice has continued.

The area around Seville is an important producer of rice, so expect to see many dishes incorporating that grain. Obviously seafood also features widely.

Following is a selection of eateries that serve reasonably -priced local cuisine.

Casa Robles, Alvarez Quintero 58, ph 421 31 50.

Enrique Becerra, Calle Garnazo 2, ph 422 70 93.

Llorens, Calle Pastor y Landero 19, ph 456 10 56.

Mesón de Pepe Cubero, Real 172, ph 416 00 10.

Le Bistrot de San Marco, Genaro Parlade 7, ph 462 94 51.

La Tuberba Dorada, José Luis Casso 18, ph 467 27 20.

Shopping

Don't expect to pick up any bargains in Seville. The shops are very attractive, but do your sums with the exchange rates and leave your credit card firmly in your wallet.

Department stores are: *El Cortes Ingles*, Plaza Duque de la Victoria, ph 422 09 31; and the less expensive *Galerias Preciados*, Plaza de la Magdalena, ph 422 20 14. The main shopping area is around the pedestrians-only *Calle Sierpes*.

Sightseeing

Seville Cathedral

Seville Cathedral was built on the site of the city's principal mosque during the period 1402 to 1506, and it is the fourth largest in the world. In fact it is the largest and richest *Gothic* cathedral in the world, and has the largest interior space of all cathedrals. Having said all that, it must be added that it is probably the gloomiest church in the world as well.

When in the cathedral it is hard to really appreciate its size because the view is restricted by the choir and the high altar, but it measures 83m wide, 95m long and 30m high.

The **Capilla Mayor** (high altar) has 36 tableaux on gilded hardwood depicting the life of Christ. It was constructed between 1482 and 1564. The **Coro** (choir) has wrought-iron grilles similar to those of the main altar, and ebony wood stalls in the Mudejar-Renaissance style.

The **Capilla Real** (Royal Chapel) was completed in 1575 and contains the tombs of many royal personages. It also has a 13th century carving depicting *La Virgen de los Reyes*, patron of Seville, made from larch wood.

In the south transept, near the Puerta de San Cristobal, is the **Monument of Christopher Columbus**, which was originally in Havana Cathedral and brought to Seville after the loss of Cuba in the Spanish-American War of 1898. Although the monument is often referred to as "Columbus' Tomb", he is not buried here, but his son's tomb is at the west end of the nave.

Throughout the church there is a plethora of priceless works of art and gold and silverware, in fact a visit is quite exhausting.

On the east side of the Cathedral is the **Giralda** (Weathercock), probably the world's most beautiful minaret and the landmark of Seville. Originally the minaret of the Great Mosque, the tower was built in 1184-1196. The bell-chamber was added in 1568 and is topped by a weathervane (giraldilla) 4m high in the shape of a female representing Faith and carrying the banner of Constantine. From the first gallery, at 70m, there are great views of the city, and of the Cathedral which can't really be viewed from anywhere else because of the surrounding buildings. Before you begin your ascent, though, make sure that the gallery's 24 bells are not due to be rung. The Giralda is open Mon-Sat 11am-5pm, Sun 2-6pm.

South of the Cathedral

South of the Cathedral is the Plaza del Triunfo, and the Casa Lonja, the former Exchange which now houses the **General Archive of the Indies**. The archive has more than four million documents relating to the discovery of, and Spanish settlement in America. Much of the material is now on computer and can be accessed by researchers, but there is a changing exhibition of actual records, usually including pages from the diaries of Christopher Columbus. It is open Mon-Fri 10am-1.00pm.

At 5 Calle Santo Tomas, on the south side of the Casa Lonja, is the Old Chapterhouse (Cilla del Cabildo Catedral) which now houses the **Museo de Arte Contemporaneo**, open Tues-Fri 10am-2pm, 5-8pm; Sat-Sun 10am-2pm. The museum has works by Miro, Tapies, Saura and Chillida, as well as local artists.

The Alcazar

The **Alcazar** is on the south-east side of the Plaza del Triunfo, and it was the stronghold of the Moorish and the later Christian kings. The present building is from the second half of the 14th century. Enter through the Puerta Principal and take the narrow passageway to the left. This leads to the *Patio de las Doncellas* (Court of the Maids of Honour), built 1369-1379, but the glazed gallery was added in the 16th century.

On the north side of the Patio is the *Salon de Carlos V*, with a beautiful ceiling. Next are the apartments of a favourite lady of Pedro the Cruel (Maria de Padilla), then the Dining Room (Comedor), then the oldest room in the Alcazar, the **Salon de Embajadores** (Hall of the Ambassadors) which dates from 1420. The rest of the ground floor is taken up with royal apartments.

The magnificent staircase from the Patio de la Monteria leads to the first floor which has the apartments of the Catholic Monarchs and some fine chapels.

The **Jardines del Alcazar** (gardens) were laid out by Charles V, and are divided by a rocaille wall. Their main attractions are an underground bath-house and the **Pabellon de Carlos V** (Pavilion) to which Felipe V added the **Apeadero** which is used for exhibitions. The Alcazares is open Mon-Sat 9am-12.45pm, 3-5pm; Sun 9am-12.45pm.

The Centre of Town

To the north of the Cathedral is the centre of town, the **Plaza San Francisco**, where once were held bullfights, tournaments and executions. The west side of the square has the Renaissance **Ayuntamiento** (Town Hall), which was commenced in 1527 and finished in 1564. The front of the building is one of the best examples of the Plateresque style.

On the west side of the Town Hall is the Plaza Nueva, and on its north side is the narrow **Calle de las Sierpes** (Street of the Snakes), the main shopping street and a pedestrian zone.

Calle Jovellanos Gallegos runs of Calle de las Sierpes, on the right, and has the church of **San Salvador** from the 16th century but remodelled in Churrigueresque style in the late 18th century. The church has works by Montanes, including an *Ecce Homo,* and a painting by Murillo.

Take Calle de Aguilas from San Salvador east to the Plaza de Pilatos, and the 16th century **Casa de Pilatos**. Legend has it that whilst in the Holy Land the Marquis of Tarifa, Don Fabrique Enriquez de Ribera, visited the ruins of Pilate's house in Jerusalem. When the Marquis returned to Seville in 1521 he decided to model his home on his own idea of what the ruins represented. It is now considered to be the grandest private residence in Seville, and is owned by the Duke of Medinaceli. Much of the house and grounds are open to the public (Mon-Fri 10am-6pm, Sat 10am-2pm) and it gives an insight into the lifestyles of the different ages.

Calle de las Sierpes as it travels north becomes Calle Amor de Dios then passes the Plaza del Duque and continues to the **Alameda de Hercules**, a wide and shady avenue with gardens and, at its south end, two granite columns from a Roman temple with statues of Hercules and Julius Caesar. These two are important to Sevillan mythology. Hercules is credited as the founder of the city; Julius Caesar with building its protective **walls**, part of which can be seen on the north side of the old town between the Puerta de Cordoba and the Puerta de la Macarena.

From the Plaza del Duque take Calle de Alfonso XII to the **Museo de Bellas Artes**. Sevillans believe this museum has the greatest art collection in Spain, which makes it painfully obvious that none of them have visited the Prado in Madrid. Nevertheless it does have a good collection, particularly of the works of the 17th century Spanish painters. Artists represented include El Greco, Pacheco, de Roelas, Zurbaran, Murillo, Velazquez and Carreno.

South of the City

To the south of the city, on the Paseo de las Delicias and leading from the Puente del Generalisimo, is the **Parque de Maria Luisa**. It is named after Maria Luisa Fernanda, sister of Queen Isabel II and duchess of the Montpensier family, who presented the gardens to the city in 1893.

The Ibero-American Exhibition of 1929-30 was held in the park, and some of the buildings remain: the Palacio Centrale, with its two 82m towers at the corners, in the **Plaza de Espana**; the Pabellon Mudejar, Pabellon Real and Palacio del Rinacimiento in the **Plaza de America**.

The Pabellon Mudejar houses the **Museum of Folk Art and Costume**, and another building in the Plaza de America houses the **Archaeological Museum**.

The International Exhibition of 1992 celebrated the 500th anniversary of the discovery of America, and was held on an island between the Guadalquivir and the Canal de Alfonso XIII, to the north of the suburb of Barrio de Triana.

The central feature of the Expo was the Carthusian monastery of Santa Maria de las Cuevas, founded in 1401. It was there that Columbus planned his voyage across the Atlantic.

Switzerland

Land-locked Switzerland has an area of 41,288 sq km and a population of 6,674,000, whose language depends on which part of the country they inhabit. Around 70% speak a dialect of German, but those who live between the French border and the Matterhorn speak French and account for another 20%. The remaining 10% is divided between the southernmost canton of Ticino where Italian is spoken, and the Engadine and Upper Rhine Valley where people speak Romansch, an ancient language of Roman origin. Most people in the hospitality industry speak English.

The government is a Confederation of twenty-three Cantons, that have their own government and administration. The Federal Government is responsible for defence, foreign affairs and transport and postal systems.

Climate

Average temperatures for Zurich are: Jan max 2C, min -3C; July max 25C, min 14C. July and August are the peak tourist months, when it is necessary to queue for every attraction and service, but June and September have roughly the same weather, less crowds, and cheaper hotel tariffs.

Entry Regulations

Visitors must have a valid passport, but a visa is not required for visits up to 90 days.

The duty free allowance is 400 cigarettes or 100 cigars or 500 gm pipe tobacco; alcoholic beverages up to 15% proof 2 litres, over 15% proof 1 litre; perfumery 0.5 litre, films unrestricted if for personal use. There is no restriction on the import or export of currency. No vaccinations are required.

Currency

The currency of the land is the Swiss Franc (SFr), which is divided into 100 centimes or rappen. Approximate exchange rates, which should be used as a guide only, are:

A$	= 1.10SFr
Can$	= 1.05SFr
NZ$	= 0.95SFr
S$	= 0.95SFr
UK£	= 2.25SFr
US$	= 1.50SFr

Notes are in denominations of 1000, 500, 100, 50, 20 and 10 Swiss Francs, and coins are 5, 2 and 1 Franc and 50, 20, 10 and 5 centimes.

Banks are open Mon-Fri 8.30am-noon, 2-4.30pm. There are no currency restrictions and at exchange offices (Bureaux de Change or Geldwechsel) most currencies can be bought or sold.

Shopping hours are Mon-Fri 8am-12.30pm, 1.30-6.30pm, Sat 8am-12.30pm, 1.30-4pm, although in the big cities the shops tend to stay open at lunch time.

Post offices are open Mon-Fri 7.30am-noon, 1.45-6pm, Sat 8.30-11am.

Credit cards are widely accepted, though it is better to have some cash when travelling through the smaller towns. There is a Goods and Services Tax (MWST) of 6.5% on most items.

Telephone

International direct dialling is available and the International code is 00, the country code 41.

It is expensive to make international calls from hotels.

Driving

It is necessary to have an international driving licence to hire a car. Driving is on the right. In this country traffic coming from the right has priority, as have trams in the cities and post-buses on mountain roads.

Speed limits are:

Motorways -   130kph;

Open roads   100kph;
built-up areas   60kmh.
On-the-spot fines can be imposed for speeding.

Miscellaneous

Local time is GMT + 1 (Central European Time). Daylight saving
operates from late March to late September.

Electricity is 220v AC, with round, two-pin plugs.
Switzerland has an excellent health system, but it is wise to have
insurance cover.

Lucerne (Luzern)

Lucerne is the capital of Central Switzerland (Zentralschweiz),
which is the most popular region of the country with tourists.
Consequently there is no shortage of hotels and restaurants in
this part of the world, and getting to Lucerne by road or rail is
easy and picturesque.
      The city is attractively situated on the banks of the Reuss
River as it begins its journey from the Vierwaldstattersee (also
called Lake Lucerne).

History

Central Switzerland, in particular the areas around
Vierwaldstattersee, is William Tell country. This legendary
national hero leapt into the lake from the wicked Gessler's boat
and escaped. His story has been told in drama and music, and
even if he did not actually exist, as historians believe, the events
taking place in the story did.
      The Rutli meadow, on the western shores of the lake, is where
representatives of the Confederates of Schwyz, Uri and
Unterwald met in 1291 to compose the Oath of Eternal Alliance,
which formed the world's oldest still existing democracy.

Tourist Information

The main information office for the city is near the Bahnhof (station) at Frankenstrasse 1, ph 51 71 71. It is open Mon-Fri 8.30am-6pm, Sat 9am-5pm (April-October) Sun 9am-1pm (May-October); Mon-Fri 8.30am-noon and 2-6pm, Sat 9am-1pm (November-March).

The main office for all of Central Switzerland of the Verkehrsverband Zentralschweiz, Alpenstrasse 1, ph 51 18 91, and it is open Mon-Fri 9am-noon, 2-5pm.

Another tourist office is found at Schweizerhofquai 2, and it is open Mon-Fri 9am-noon, 1-7pm, Sat 9am-4pm (May and October); Mon-Fri 9am-5pm, Sat 9am-4pm (June-September).

Local Transport

There are efficient bus and trolley bus services.

Accommodation

Chateau Gutsch, Kanonenstrasse, ph (41) 220 272, fax (41) 220 252, was built as an hotel in 1888, but you could be forgiven for thinking that it was originally a castle. Expensive, but great for a once-in-a-lifetime experience.

Drei Konige, Bruchstrasse 35, ph (41) 228 833, is close to the bridges of the old town. Has a restaurant, but many prefer to walk to the Galliker for dinner.

Schlussel, Franziskanerplatz 12, ph (41) 231 061, is one of the more reasonable hotels in Lucerne, and consequently usually has young people as guests. Facilities include a breakfast room.

Lucerne's youth hostel is at Seledstrasse 12, ph (41) 368 800, fax (41) 365 696.

Food and Drink

The specialty of Lucerne is Kugelipaschtetli, puff-pastry filled with chicken, veal or sweetbreads, mushrooms and cream sauce. Fish is also prominent on the city's menus, usually sauteed and served with tomato, mushroom and caper sauce.

Restaurants around here are not cheap, although the food is very good and so you often feel the price justified.

Here are a few at the lower end of the price scale.

Zur Pfistern, Kornmarkt 4, ph 51 36 50 - a 14th century guildhall on the old-town waterfront - fish dishes are recommended - credit cards accepted.

Rebstock/Hofstube, St Leodegarstrasse 3, ph 51 35 81 (next to the Hofkirche)—international cuisine in brasserie and the more formal restaurant, reservations necessary, credit cards accepted
Galliker, Schutzenstrasse 1, ph 22 10 02 - real traditional Luzerner cuisine - popular with locals and visitors - reservations a good idea - credit cards accepted. Note: This restaurant is closed on Sunday and Monday from mid-July to mid-August.

Shopping
Lucerne is the main shopping venue for the entire region, so the shops tend to remain open longer than in other cities.

The main department store is Jelmoli, Pilatusstrasse 4, ph 24 22 11, and the chain stores are Nordmann, Weggisgasse 5, ph 50 22 66, and EPA, Rossligasse 20, ph 51 19 77.

Lucerne was once a major producer of lace and embroidery goods, but although this is no longer the case, it is still one of the best places to buy Swiss handwork. Watches are also high on people's shopping lists.
For lace and embroidered goods try:
Sturzenegger, Schwanenplatz 7, ph 51 19 58;
Schmid-Linder, Denkmalstrasse 9, ph 51 43 46;
Innerschweizer Heimatwerk, Franziskanerplatz 14, ph 23 69 44.
For watches try:
Bucherer, Schwanenplatz, ph 43 77 00, who represents Piaget and Rolex; and *Gubelin,* Schweizerhofquai, ph 51 51 42, who represents Philippe, Patek, and Audemars Piguet as well as its own brand.

Sightseeing

A walking tour
It can begin at the **Altes Rathaus** (Old Town Hall) which was built in the late Renaissance style between 1599 and 1606, and has been used by the town council for its meetings since 1606. It is on Rathausquai, facing the modern bridge, **Rathaus-Steg**.

On the right of the Town Hall, in Furrengasse, is the **Am Rhyn Haus**, which has a good collection of Picasso paintings from his late period. It is open daily 10am-6pm (Jan-Oct); 11am-1pm, 2-4pm (Nov-Mar).

Take the stairs on the right, and pass the Zunfthaus zu Pfistern, a guildhall and restaurant, to the Kornmarkt. Cross the square and go to the left into the **Weinmarkt**, the most picturesque of the city's squares. During the 15th, 16th and 17th centuries people came from all over Europe to see the famous passion plays presented in this square, which before that time was the site of the wine market. The fountain in the centre portrays St Mauritius, the patron saint of warriors.

Now walk towards the **Spreuerbrucke**, the narrow wooden bridge that runs off Muhlenplatz. The bridge dates from 1408 and its inside gables have a series of 17th century paintings by Kaspar Meglinger of the Dance of Death. They are well preserved, but certainly not to everyone's taste.

The other end of the bridge brings you to the **Natur-Museum** and next to it the **Historisches Museum**. The Natural History Museum has very modern exhibits and even some live animals. It is in Kasernenplatz, ph 24 54 11, and is open Tues-Sat 10-noon, 2-5pm; Sun 10am-5pm. The Historical Museum, in Pfistergasse, ph 24 54 24, is not really very interesting to anyone who is not Swiss, but nevertheless it is open Tues-Fri 10am-noon, 2-5pm; Sat-Sun 10am-5pm.

Continue along Pfistergasse in the direction of the lake until you get to Bahnhofstrasse, turn left, then right into Munzgasse. Continue on to Franziskanerplatz and the **Franziskanerkirche** (Franciscan Church), which is more than 700 years old although it has been renovated more than a few times and lost a lot of its original style.

Go back to Bahnhofstrasse, turn right and walk past the Government Building (**Regierungsgebaude**), the home of the cantonal government, to the **Jesuitenkirche** (Jesuit Church). This church was built between 1667 and 1678, and is worth a visit. The enormous interior has been completely restored and it is a brilliant example of the Rococo style. Next door, in Theaterstrasse, is the **Stadttheater** (City Theatre), ph 23 66 19. On the waterfront there is a fish market every Friday morning.

Next we cross the 14th century **Kapellbrucke** (Chapel Bridge), the oldest wooden bridge in Europe. Bridges usually go across rivers in a straight line, but not this one - it crosses diagonally. This is because it originally was a division between the river and the lake. The bridge is the symbol of Lucerne - its stone water tower, its shingled roof and its shape making it instantly recognizable, much as the Golden Gate to San Francisco and the Harbour Bridge to Sydney.

When you walk across you will notice the gables painted by Heinrich Wagman in the 17th century, but some will be empty. There were 112 panels depicting local history, legends and coats of arms, but during a fire in 1993, 78 of the paintings were completely destroyed, and some others are being carefully restored and will be replaced. The bill for rebuilding and restoring the bridge came to around 3 million Swiss francs.

From the bridge veer towards your right through the Schwanenplatz and along Schweizerhofquai, passing the Hotel Schweizerhof, which has had as guests Napoleon III, Mark Twain, Leo Tolstoy and Richard Wagner. Continue to Zurichstrasse, turn left and continue to Lowenplatz where you can't miss the **Bourbaki-Panorama**.

A conical structure built as a tourist attraction and nothing else, has a panoramic painting of the French Army retreating into Switzerland during the Franco-Prussian War. As you walk around the painting seems to become 3-D with things coming out towards to you. There is also a recorded commentary in several languages and the whole is open daily 9am-6pm (May-Sept), 9am-5pm (March-April and October).

The well-known restaurant, the Old Swiss House, is next door to the Panorama, but check out the prices before you wander in.

Lowendenkmal
From Lowenplatz take Denkmalstrasse to the **Lowendenkmal** (Lion Monument), another symbol of Lucerne that should not be missed under any circumstances. It is carved out of a sheer sandstone face and is a dying lion, with a broken spear in his side and his chin sagging on his shield. Carved by Lucas Ahorn of Konstanz, from a design by Danish sculptor Berthel

Thorwaldsen, it commemorates 760 Swiss guards, and their officers, who were killed defending Louis XVI at the Tuileries in Paris in 1792. There is a Latin inscription that translates: "To the bravery and fidelity of the Swiss". When you are there, standing near the pond in front of the monument, take a moment to look at people around you. Many will have tears in their eyes, not because they feel any affinity with some brave men who died over two hundred years ago, but simply because of the spirit evoked by the carving itself.

Next to the park that houses the Lion is the **Gletschergarten** (Glacier Garden), where excavations between 1872 and 1875 revealed bedrock that had been polished and pocked by glaciers during the Ice Age. A small museum on site has impressive relief maps of Switzerland, but admission times vary dramatically so ph 51 43 40 for information.

To get back to the city centre, return to Lowenplatz, get back onto Zurichstrasse, then turn right onto Museggstrasse and follow it all the way. It actually goes through one of the 15th century city gates, and gives some good views of the old town.

Zurich

The largest city in Switzerland, Zurich has a population of around 400,000 and is situated on the Limmat River and along the shores of the northern tip of the Zurichsee (see = lake).

Zurich is a very beautiful city, and a commercial, industrial and university centre. One could be forgiven for wondering why it is not the capital of Switzerland, but that honour goes to Bern.

History

It is known that the area was inhabited as early as 4500BC, for land and marine archaeologists have discovered artifacts from many Stone Age and Iron Age settlements around the lake.

The Romans, ever on the lookout for a good, central location, built a customs house on a hill overlooking the river in the 1st century BC. The customs house became a fortress, and remains of it can still be seen. Legend has it that the Romans were also responsible for providing Zurich with its patron saints. During the Roman occupation, a brother and sister, Felix and Regula, were beheaded by the Roman governor because they were Christians. That part is historically correct, but the rest has yet to be proven. After their execution they picked up their heads, waded through the water, and marched up a hill before succumbing at a spot where the Grossmunster now stands.

The Romans were ousted in the 5th century by the ancestors of the present occupants, but the importance of the town dwindled until four hundred years later when the Carolingians built an imperial palace on the banks of the Limmat. Then Louis the German, grandson of Charlemagne, had an abbey built where the Fraumunster now stands.

Zurich's flair for trade and commerce was evident by the 12th century, and the merchants became very powerful. This was not appreciated by the tradesmen and labourers who, led by an aristocrat named Rudolf Brun, took the merchants on, and defeated the town council. They then established the guilds for which Zurich is famous, and in fact the original thirteen guilds retained their power until the French Revolution. They still have their prestige, shown by the annual festival when businessmen don medieval costumes for the procession through the city to the guildhalls.

During the Reformation a leader named Huldrych Zwingli preached in the Grossmunster, exhorting the populace to thrift and hard work. His success can be measured by the fact that the Zurich stock exchange is the fourth most important in the world (after New York, London and Tokyo) and turns over on average 636 billion Swiss Francs each year.

Tourist Information

The tourist information office as at Bahnhofplatz 15, ph 211 4000, and it is open Mon-Fri 8.30am-9.30pm, Sat-Sun 8.30am-8.30pm (April-October; Mon-Fri 8.30am-7.30pm, Sat-Sun 8.30am-6.30pm (November-March).

Local Transport

Zurich has a very efficient tram service from 5.30am to midnight. Tickets must be purchased from vending machines before boarding.

Taxis are not really an alternative as they are very expensive - 8 SFr minimum.

Accommodation

Dolder Grand, Kurhausstrasse 65, ph (1) 251 6231, fax (1) 251 8829 is a picturesque, 5-star hotel. Facilities include restaurant, bar, coffee shop, swimming pool, golf course, tennis courts, ice-skating rink, beauty salon.

Neues Schloss, Stockerstrasse 17, ph (1) 201 6550, fax (1) 201 6418, is a small hotel in the business district. Facilities include Le Jardin restaurant.

Rossli, Rossligasse 7, ph (1) 252 2121, fax (1) 252 2131, is situated near the Grossmunster in Oberdorf, and is very modern in decor. Prices are reasonable and facilities include breakfast rooms and a bar.

Zurich's youth hostel is *Wollishofen*, Mutschellenstrasse 114, ph (1) 482 3544, fax (1) 481 9992.

Food and Drink

A few dishes spring to mind when thinking of Switzerland - cheese fondue, rosti and veal in cream and white wine sauce. Everyone knows of the first and last, but rosti might be new to some. It is a cake of hash-brown potatoes crisped in a skillet and flavoured with bacon, herbs or cheese. And it is delicious.

The Swiss use a lot of cheese in their main courses, and a lot of chocolate in their desserts. Speaking of chocolate, it is available everywhere and is simply the best, though it is not cheap. Actually, eating anything in Switzerland, and in Zurich particularly, is an expensive exercise. Probably the best bet is to have the main meal at lunch-time and take advantage of the reduced prices for business lunches.

Here are a few restaurants that won't charge an arm and leg:

Zeughauskeller, Bahnhofstrasse 23, ph 211 26 90 - 15th century building that is popular with locals and visitors alike - reservations necessary for lunch - no credit cards accepted.

Mere Catherine, Nagelihof 3, ph 262 22 50 - bistro with a varied menu and an interesting clientele - no credit cards accepted.

Rheinfelder Bierhaus, Marktgasse 19, ph 251 29 91 - somewhat dreary decor but excellent home-made meals. They do not accept credit cards.

Shopping

The main department stores are *Jelmoli*, Bahnhofstrasse at Seidengasse, ph 220 44 11, and *Globus*, Bahnhofstrasse at Lowenplatz, ph 221 33 11. Smaller chain stores are *Vilan*, Bahnhofstrasse 75, ph 229 51 11 and *ABM*, Bellevueplatz, ph 261 44 84.

The main shopping street, as you may have worked out for yourself, is **Bahnhofstrasse** and the Paradeplatz end, towards the lake, has the more exclusive shops and boutiques.

A flea market is held every Saturday 6am-3.30pm at Burkliplatz, which is at the lake end of Bahnhofstrasse.

Sightseeing

The main sights of Zurich are easily seen on a walking tour and the best place to begin is the Hauptbahnhof (Main Railway Station). When the enormous station was first built, in the 1800s, it was considered to be a work of beauty. Time has taken its toll. The current restoration program has been going on for some time. It is expected to be even grander than before.

The **Schweizerisches Landesmuseum** (Swiss National Museum) is at Museumstrasse 2, behind the station, in a huge Gothic building. Exhibits include Stone Age objects, early watches, dress and furniture from earlier times, and models of military battles. A mural by Ferdinand Hodler entitled *Retreat of the Swiss Confederates at Marignano* is in the hall of arms. The museum is open Tues-Sun 10am-5pm and admission is free.

The statue in the centre of Bahnhofplatz is of **Alfred Escher**, a financial wizard and politician who was responsible for Zurich becoming a major banking centre. He was also involved in the development of the city's university, the Federal Railways and the tunnel under the St Gotthard Pass.

There is a subterranean passage under Bahnhofplatz that comes out at **Bahnhofstrasse**, the city's main street and principal shopping strip.

Continue along this street until you come to Rennweg, on the left. Turn into it and then left again onto Fortunagasse, then continue on to the **Lindenhof** square. Here there are remains of the Roman fortress and a medieval imperial residence. There is also a fountain that commemorates the women of Zurich who, in 1292, saved the town from the Hapsburgs. Apparently the town was all but defeated when the women donned uniforms and armour and marched to the Lindenhof. When the enemy saw them coming they assumed that it was a second, fresh army and so fled the scene.

A short walk from here to your right takes you to the St Peterhof and **St Peterskirche**, the oldest parish church in Zurich. There has been a church on this site since the 9th century, but the present building dates only from the 13th century. In the tower is the largest clock face in Europe. Again walking to your right, turn into Schlusselgasse, then into an alley named Thermengasse. Through grates you will be able to see beneath you the ruins of **Roman baths**, which have recently been excavated. There are signs giving details of the dig. Continue on to **Weinplatz** which has some excellent shops, and opens onto the riverside. After checking out the shops, continue on your way, crossing the Rathaus Bridge over the river.

The street that runs along the riverbank on this side is called **Limmat Quai** and near here at nos. 40, 42 and 54 there are some interesting guildhalls (zunfthausen) that are now restaurants. No. 40 is **Zunfthaus zur Zimmerleuten** which dates from 1708 and was for carpenters; no. 42 is **Gesellschaftshaus zum Ruden** a 13th century noblemen's hall; and no. 54 is **Zunfthaus zur Saffran** a 14th century haberdashers' meeting place.

Across from no. 54 is the 17th century Baroque **Rathaus** (Town Hall), which can only be visited by people attending the cantonal Parliament Monday morning meeting, or the city Parliament Wednesday afternoon meeting. The interior is in good condition and the stucco ceiling in the Banquet Hall is worth a look.

Further along Limmat Quai is the 15th century **Wasserkirche** (Water Church) built in the late-Gothic style with stained glass by Giacometti. Attached to the church is the **Helmhaus** which dates from the 18th century. Here a linen market was once held, but now it has changing contemporary art exhibitions. It is open Tues-Sun 10am-6pm (until 9pm Thurs), and for more information ph 251 71 66. Both these buildings were once on an island, the one where Felix and Regula lost their heads.

Continuing towards the lake the next stop is the very grand **Grossmunster**. The church was built on the site of a Carolingian church which was dedicated to Felix and Regula, as this was where they carried their heads to, and where they were buried. Legend has it that Charlemagne decided that a church should be built on the spot when his horse stumbled over their graves. There is a huge statue of Charlemagne near the south tower, but it is only a copy - the original is in the crypt for safe-keeping. The inside of the church is very austere, but remember that this was where Zwingli preached his 'thrift and hard work' sermons.

Follow Limmat Quai to Ramistrasse, and if you are interested in art, turn left and continue on to the **Kunsthaus** (Art Gallery) on Heimplatz. It is open Tues-Thurs 10am-9pm, Sat-Sun 10am-5pm, ph 251 67 55. Also on Heimplatz is the **Schauspielhaus** (Theatre), which was the only German-language theatre in the world that was not controlled from Berlin during the second world war.

If you are not interested in art, turn right onto Ramistrasse, and on Bellevueplatz is the **Opern Haus** (Opera House), built in 1890 and renovated between 1980 and 1984.

As you continue across **Quai Brucke** (Bridge) take time to notice the great views both to the right of the city, and to the left of the lake. The views are particularly good at night, so a return visit is a good idea.

At the end of the bridge veer to the right, then take the second street on the right, Fraumunsterstrasse, which leads, of course, to the **Fraumunster**. Built on the site of a 9th century abbey, whose remains can be seen, the Fraumunster was originally Gothic in style, then in 1732 the beautiful narrow spires were added. The Romanesque choir has stained-glass windows by Marc Chagall.

At Munsterhof 20 is the Baroque **Zunfthaus zur Meisen**, an 18th century guildhall for the wine merchants that now houses the Landesmuseum's ceramics collection, ph 221 21 44. Open Tues-Fri and Sun 10am-noon, 2-5pm, Sat 10am-noon, 2-4pm. Also in this square is the **Zunfthaus zur Waag**, a 17th century guildhall for the linen weavers and hat makers.

Walk along Poststrasse to Paradeplatz, a major crossroads and centre on Bahnhofstrasse, from where you can catch a train back to the railway station, or wherever you are staying.

United Kingdom

The countries which make up the United Kingdom, also called Great Britain, are England, Scotland, Wales and Northern Ireland and cover an area of 244,100 sq km with a total population of 58,123,000.

Not much is known about English history before the invasion by Julius Caesar in 55BC making it a Roman province. The last Roman legions were withdrawn in 442AD leaving behind many temples, baths, forums, walls and paved highways which can still be seen today.

Peace was short-lived. The warring Picts and Scots from the north continually invaded. The Welsh also attacked England.

King Edward l of England subdued the Welsh and his son, the first Prince of Wales was born at Caernarvon in 1284. This did not quell the rebellions but Henry Vlll finally joined the two countries under the same system of laws and government.

The Romans tried unsuccessfully to capture Scotland but finally gave up and built a wall across the north of England. Scotland became united with England in 1603 when Mary Queen of Scots' son, James Vl of Scotland became James l of England.

England, Scotland and Wales became united in 1707 under Queen Anne to form Great Britain.

Religious disputes have plagued Ireland since its beginning. Northern Ireland has always been largely Protestant. This was resented by the Catholic Irish of the south. The rebellion of 1641 lasted 8 years and paved the way for Oliver Cromwell to conquer the entire island. In 1916 Sin Féin declared southern Ireland an independent state. After an impossible conflict for the British, Britain withdrew her troops and in 1921 the Irish Free State was proclaimed. Later the south became the Republic of Ireland and the north remained under British rule with a

guaranteed protestant majority in political life. A vexed political situation that has to be addressed.

Latest available population figures are: England 46,382,050, Scotland 4,962,152, Wales 2,811,865. English is spoken throughout the United Kingdom. However, Gaelic is also spoken in some parts of Scotland. The Welsh also maintain their ancient Celtic tongue.

Climate

On the whole Britain has a cool climate. January is the coldest month with temperatures of 4C (39F). July and August are the warmest 16C (60F). The highest rainfall is in November with 97 mm. **September is considered by many to be the best time of the year to visit.** The temperature is 57F (14C), rainfall 3.2 ins (83 mm); there are less tourists to compete with; and prices fall. Tourist attractions and some hotels close at the end of September until Easter. **April and May are also good months to visit.** The spring flowers are in bloom and the temperature is reasonable.

Entry Regulations

All visitors must produce a valid passport. Commonwealth visitors staying less than six months do not require a visa. No vaccinations are required.

The duty free allowance is 200 cigarettes or 100 cigarillos or 50 cigars or 250gm tobacco. Alcoholic drinks: 2 litres of still wine plus 1 litre of drinks over 22% vol, or 2 litres of alcoholic drinks under 22% vol or a further 2 litres of still wine. 50gms perfume, 250cc of toilet water. Other goods worth £32.

Currency

The currency of the land is the British Pound (£), which is divided into 100 pence. Approximate exchange rates, which should be used as a guide only, are:

A$	= £0.45
Can$	= £0.43
NZ$	= £0.40
S$	= £0.43
US$	= £0.60

Notes are in denominations of £50, £20, £10, £5, and coins are £1, 50p, 20p, 10p, 5p, 2p and 1p.

Scotland has its own notes and although English pounds are accepted in Scotland, you must change your Scottish pounds before you leave that part of the country. They are the same value and denomination as the English.

Major credit cards are accepted but not by some leading stores. You can obtain money from certain banks with your card. Check before leaving home as to which bank takes your card.

Changing travellers cheques can be expensive. There is a £3.50 commission charge at most banks and money exchanges. American Express travellers cheques can be changed free of commission at Lloyds and the Bank of Scotland. Thomas Cooks cheques at Thomas Cook outlets.

Banks are open Mon-Fri 9.30am-3.30pm (Northern Ireland 10am-3.30pm). Some major banks open on Saturday mornings. Closed Public Holidays and Sundays. Some banks in Scotland and Northern Ireland close for an hour at lunchtime.

Post offices are open Mon-Fri 9am-5.30pm, Sat 9am-12.30 pm. **If you don't have anywhere to have mail sent the best address is *Poste Restante*, Trafalgar Square Branch, 24-28 William IV Street, London WC2N 4DL. They will hold your mail for four weeks. You must show proof of identity to collect it.

Shopping Hours

Most shops open at 9.30am and close at 6pm, Mon-Sat. Small shops usually open at 9am. Late night shopping is Thursday when shops stay open until 8pm. Harrods opens at 10am until 7pm. In suburbs many shops close for a half day on Wednesday or Thursday. In the country they often close for lunch.

Tax

VAT (value added tax) 17.5% is charged on most goods and services. Non-EC residents may reclaim VAT but it has to be arranged through shops. Not all retailers participate and the value of the item is also considered. The goods must be produced to customs at your port of exit from Europe along with a form which the store will have given you. Shops usually charge a fee for the service. In other words, unless you have done some very expensive shopping it is not worth the trouble.

Telephone

It will cost more to phone from your hotel. Go to a pay phone. As a considerable amount of small change is needed to make even a local call, it is better to buy a phonecard. These are available from any British Tourist Information Centre, post offices and shops displaying the green phonecard sign. They come in £2, £4, £10 or £20 credit. For Overseas calls dial 010 then the country code, the area code then the number. Check the time difference in the phone book.

Driving

Driving is on the left-hand side of the road. The wearing of seat belts is compulsory. There are strong penalties for driving while under the influence of alcohol. Take your driving licence with you. People from certain countries only require their current licence. They can drive on it for one year. Countries not exempt need an International Driving Permit obtainable in your home town. Check before you leave home.

Road signs are almost all international. A copy of the highway code is obtainable from the AA, RAC, airports and car rental firms. The speed limit

30mph (48kph) -	in built up areas,
40mph -	in some suburban areas
70mph (113kph) -	on motorways
and 60mph (97kph) -	on other roads.

Parking can be a headache. Not allowed where there is an unbroken yellow line. Broken yellow or red lines indicate no stopping. As there are few parking meters it is safer to go into a parking area where you put your money in a machine. If you park illegally, the authorities will clamp your wheels and you will have to pay a hefty fine—twenty-four hour incnvenience!

Miscellaneous

Local time is GMT. Daylight saving operates from late March to late September.

Electricity is 240v AC. Take an adaptor or converter with you as the plugs are a different shape.

Health - Take any medication you require with you. It is also advisable to photocopy your prescriptions. Ask your doctor to give you a letter listing all medications you are on and any ailment from which you may suffer. If you have a metal hip you will probably set off the machine in airport security. Keep all medication in your overnight bag. It is essential to be covered for health insurance. It is also advisable to carry full insurance in case of emergencies.

Disabled facilities - Britain caters for the disabled. Most hotels and B&B have walk in showers and ground floor rooms. British Rail and London Underground assist passengers on and off trains. With British Rail you must notify them the day before you travel. In the underground simply ask one of the staff for assistance. Advice can be obtained from Holiday Care Service, 2 Old Bank Chambers, Station Road, Horley, Surry, ph (0293) 774 535. Ask the British Tourist Authority for a Holiday Care enquiry form.

Pubs

Drinking hours are 11am-11pm weekdays, Sun 11am-3pm, 7-10pm. Times can vary according to area. All pubs serve food ranging from sandwiches and snacks to full hot dinners. There is no VAT on pub food which is of excellent quality.

Restaurants usually have a menu outside with the prices. It is advisable to check this before entering. Remember to add the VAT and, in most cases, there is also a service charge.

Tipping

If an hotel or restaurant adds a service charge to your bill, there is no need to tip. Taxi drivers expect 10%, porters 50p a bag. Tipping is not so popular as in the past and is now confined to those who give extra service.

London

London is a huge metropolis with a population of about 7,000,000 plus a floating population of workers and tourists. It has something for everyone.

History

The oldest part is the city of London a small square-mile patch, the original Roman Londinium. Although it is really the banking and commercial sector it also has some of the main tourist attractions. The City of Westminster is also another sector where many of the attractions can be found. Next you have the West End where the theatres and shops are located. After these main areas, London stretches out in every direction.

The Romans built their city at the highest point of the Thames. It was started on Cornhills and Ludgate Hill. It was sacked by Bodicea in AD 61 and attacked by the Vikings.

William the Conqueror built the White Tower of the Tower of London in the 11th century. The church and the 'guilds' sponsored building during the Middle Ages. St Bartholomew the Great 1123, St John of Jerusalem, Clerkenwell 1150, Temple Church 1185. Westminster Abbey was started in the 11th century. Southwick Cathedral, Westminster Hall, Lambeth Palace and the Guildhall were all built during this century.

By the 16th century, London had started to expand and St James Palace was erected. Queens House, Greenwich 1619-35, Banqueting Hall, Whitehall 1619-22 which has ceilings painted by Rubens. St Pauls Cathedral was built in 1665 and destroyed by fire in 1666. The Cathedral was replaced by Wren.

The 17th and 18th century saw more expansion with numerous squares designed by the Adams Brothers. These included Adelphi, Strand and Portland Place.

London was badly bombed during World War II but the damage has been repaired, with some historical buildings being replaced by modern office blocks.

Tourist Information

British Tourist Authority has its head office in Lower Regent

Street. You can make reservations for transport, accommodation and theatre; change money, buy phonecards or shop for souvenirs. BTA information centres are located at all major railway stations.

Local Transport

You can go almost anywhere on the underground. Maps show you which route to take. Buses are frequent but because of the traffic, are not as fast. There are also Green Line buses to places outside the metropolitan area. Trains go in every direction. Travel passes are available for trains, coaches and the underground. They must be purchased before you leave home. London underground and bus passes can be purchased for 3, 4 or 7 days. They enable you to travel at any time during the period. Normally, cheap excursion fares cannot be bought before 9.30am. A London travel card can be obtained, after you arrive, at Underground stations. For this you will need to provide a passport size photograph.

Taxis are plentiful and on the whole reasonably priced. A taxi driver expects a 10% tip.

One of the best ways for a visitor to see London is on a **London Transport Sightseeing Bus**. These double deckers also give photographers plenty of scope. They can be taken from Haymarket, Trafalgar Square, Victoria station and Baker Street station. You can buy your ticket on board but if you purchase it in advance from one of the Travel Information Centres you will save £1. If you buy your ticket from the Travel Centre in either Oxford Circus or Piccadilly undergrounds you will save £2.

London Plus bus leaves every half an hour. It makes over 30 stops and you can get off, look at the sights then catch the next bus. Like the original sightseeing bus, you can save £2 by buying your ticket at Oxford Circus or Piccadilly Circus undergrounds.

Accommodation

Deluxe

Waldorf, Aldwych WC2B 4DD, ph (071) 836-7244, fax (071) 856-7244 - 292 rooms, restaurant, bars. palm court, pub, wheelchair access. Close for those doing genealogy. Single

£170-200. Double £170-£210.

Ritz, Piccadilly WIV 9D6, phone (071) 493-8181, fax (071) 493-2687 - 129 rooms. Stately, luxury hotel (noted for afternoon tea) decorated in the French style. Restaurant, bars, romantic Italian al fresco dining room. Handy to everything, transport at the door. Single £161 double £187-£239.

Hyde Park, 66 Knightsbridge SW1Y 7LA, ph (071) 235-2000, fax (071) 235-4552 - 185 rooms. Convenient to Harrods, Hyde Park and West End. One mile from Victoria station, buses and underground at door. Restaurant, bars, gym, laundry service, baby sitting. A charge for parking. Single £165-£275, double £225-£275.

Moderate

Crescent, 49-50 Cartwright Gardens WC1H 9EL, ph (071) 387-1515, fax (071) 383-2054 - 28 rooms (some with private facilities). Comfortable, friendly, full breakfast, TV lounge. Situated between Euston and Russel Square tubes. Luggage minded until you return. B&B single £34.50-£40 double £50.50-£63.

London Tourist Hotel, 13 Penywern Road, Earls Court SW5 9TT, ph (071) 370-4356, fax (071) 370-7923 - 32 rooms with private facilities, TV, phone. On route to Heathrow and Piccadilly. B&B single £39-£42 double £54-£59.

Royal Adelphi, 21 Villiers Street, WC2N 6ND, ph (071) 930 8764, fax (071) 930-8735 - 50 bedrooms (some with private facilities), TV, phone, bar, 24hr reception, continental breakfast. Next to Charing Cross Station and Strand. B&B Single £35-£50 double £50-£60.

Inexpensive

Glynne Court Hotel, 41 Great Cumberland Place, Marble Arch, W1H 7GH, ph (071) 2624-344. Friendly hotel 3 minutes walk from Marble Arch, Oxford Street, near theatres - 12 rooms - B&B single £30, double £40.

Green Court Hotel, 52 Hogarth Road, SW5 0PU, ph (071) 370 0853 - 23 rooms (some with private facilities), Near Earls Court station. Single £18-£25 double £25-30.

Luna-Simone House 47 Belgrave Road, SW1V 2BB, ph (071) 834-5897 - 35 rooms. Near Victoria Coach Station. Friendly, full breakfast. B&B single £18-£24 double £30-£48.

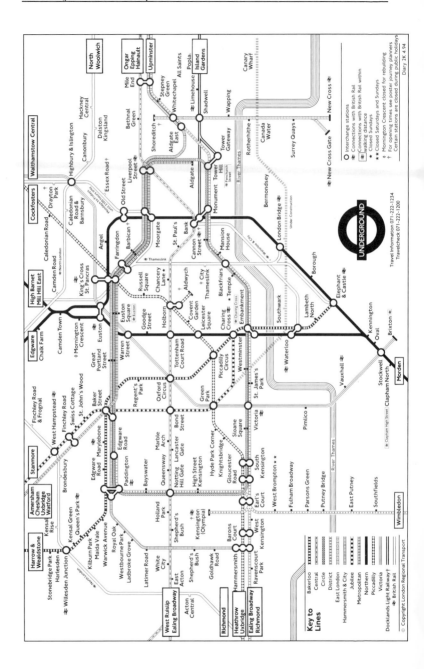

Food and Drink

Think of dining out in London and you will probably think of fish and chips, or bangers and mash, washed down with a pint of ale. These are still available, of course, but every other type of food you can imagine can also be found in London.

Beware of restaurants, though, with well-known names such as the Savoy, Suntory, or the Ivy. They are all excruciatingly expensive. Look at the menu outside before you enter. For best value go to the pubs, or British Home Stores and Littlewoods have cafeterias at reasonable prices.

Sightseeing

The main tourist attractions are:
In the city of London, **St Paul's Cathedral** where you can see tombs of the famous in the crypt and climb to the dome where you can whisper to a friend at the other end of the whispering gallery and they will hear you. Take the underground to St Pauls station. Open Mon-Sat 8.30am-4pm; Galleries 10am-4.15pm, admission to Cathedral and crypt £3 adult, £2 child; to galleries £2.50 adult, £1.50 child.

See the medieval **Guildhall** where the City Council meets: the **Old Bailey**, built on the site of the infamous Newgate prison, is where most of the famous criminals have been brought to justice. Seats in the public galleries are very much sort after so be early. Close to the Old Bailey is the "Old Lady of Threadneedle Street", more formally known as the Bank of England. You can see the lane where the fire of London started, visit pubs frequented by Bacon, Dickens and many more but the most impressive building in the city is the **Tower of London**. The White Tower was built in the time of William the Conqueror. The Bloody Tower is where the Princes were murdered by King Richard lll. On the brighter side you can see the crown jewels displayed in well illuminated glass cases. Underground is the quickest way to the Tower - Tower station. Open 9am-6pm, entry £7.95 adult, £5.95 child.

By contrast the **City of Westminster** has wide streets with parklands. Here you can visit the **Houses of Parliament**, see the spot where Charles I was condemned to death in the **Palace** of Westminster next door (Westminster station).

Westminster Abbey stands across the road. Here all the kings and queens except Edward V and Edward Vlll have been crowned. Many famous poets, statesmen and royalty have been buried here (St James station). Open Mon-Fri 9.20am-4.45pm. Admission to Royal Chapels and Poet's Corner £4 adult, £1 child.

Stroll up Northumberland Avenue past the many offices which house the Admiralty, War Office and Foreign Office to the **Cenotaph** and into **Downing Street** where the Prime Minister lives. In the last street on the right, just before **Trafalgar Square** there is a pub called the Sherlock Holmes which serves excellent meals. It also has a museum of Sherlock Homes memorabilia.

Once in Trafalgar Square you will see the tall column with **Lord Nelson** on the top. **St Martin's-in-the-Fields** church, the **National Gallery** and the **Reference Library** are all here. Through the **Admiralty Arch** you come to the **Mall** with **Buckingham Palace** at the end. Don't miss the **Changing of the Guard**. For times ring (0839) 123 456.

Those interested in World War II, should visit the **Cabinet War Rooms** where Winston Churchill and his cabinet made their decisions. Clive Steps, King Charles Street,(Westminster station). Open 10am-6pm, admission £3.90 adult, £1.90 child.

Take the underground to Baker Street, turn into Marylebone Road and visit **Madame Tussauds** waxworks. See the famous and infamous. Have a ride in a "time taxi" through London's history. Open Mon-Fri 10am-5.30pm, Sat 9.30am-5.30pm. Admission is £8.24 adult, £5.25 child.

Museums
The British Museum and British Library has over ninety galleries. It is in Great Russell Street. Take the Underground to Tottenham Court Road or Russell Square. Open Mon-Sat 10am-5pm, Sun 2.30-6pm, and there is no admission fee.

　　Dickens House Museum is in Doughty (Russell Square station) and contains a comprehensive Dickens library. Open Mon-Sat 10am-5pm. Admission is £3 adult, £1 child.

　　The **Museum of London** is one of the world's largest museums. It's at London Wall (St Pauls station). Open Tues-Sat 10am -5.50pm, Sun noon-5.50pm. Admission—£3.50adult,£1.75 child.

The **Victoria and Albert Museum**, Cromwell Road (South Kensington station) is open Mon noon-5.50pm, Tues-Sun 10am-5.50pm and admission is by donation of £4.50 adult, £1 child over 12. It is a museum of decorative arts, and includes treasures from entire furnished rooms to forks and trinkets.

Kensington Palace is in Kensington Gardens (Queensway or High Street Kensington stations). The State Apartments can be visited by guided tour only. Open Mon-Sat 9am-5pm. Admission is £4.50 adult, £3 child. William and Mary took up residence here in 1689. There are often displays of special occasion clothes worn by the present Royals.

One of the best ways to see London is on foot.
You find plaques on houses, commemorating famous personages who lived there, in almost every street. Sundays are always dull but not in London. Take the underground to **Hampstead**. Walk up the hill towards the heath and look at the pavement artists. Have lunch at one of the famous pubs, for example **Jack Straws Castle** frequented by Dick Turpin the Highwayman, or stroll across the heath to the **Spaniards** also the haunt of highwaymen. The **Bull and Bush**, well known by the song, has been rebuilt. Across the road is **Anna Pavlova's house** in Golders Hill park where deer roam. Museums, art galleries and many other attractions are all open on Sundays.

Covent Garden is at its liveliest at weekends. Singers and other artists entertain you in front of **St Paul's Church**. This is known as the Actor's church and many memorials are found inside. The former wholesale fruit and vegetable market now has shops and a market which has some interesting goods at reasonable prices. The **London Transport Museum**, The **Theatre Museum** are both open. Just around the corner stands the **Royal Opera House** and **Drury Lane** theatre. For those who prefer horticulture, take the underground to Kew and wander around **Kew Gardens**. There is plenty of night life. Clubs, discos, cabarets, but do try and take in a theatre or concert.

Sights Further Afield

It is possible to go by Green line bus or a tour to visit **Windsor Castle**, open Mon-Sat 10am-4pm, Sun 2-4pm. Admission is £8 adult, £4 child, Queen's Dolls House £1.50 adult, 70p child. **Windsor station** is well worth a visit. They have a model of Queen Victoria arriving by train. **Eton school** is close to the castle.

Runnymede, where King John signed the Magna Carter in 1215, is easier to reach on a tour or by car. (Nearest station Stains.) **Hampton Court Palace** is well worth a visit, open Mon 10.15am-4.30pm, Tues Sun 9.30am-4.30pm. Admission is £7 adult, £4.70 child. **Canterbury**, **Woburn Abbey** and many more places of interest are all within easy reach.

York

North-west of London is the walled city of **York** with a population of 99,787. Its Latin name was Eboracum. Cars are not permitted inside the city walls. It was founded by the Romans in 71AD, however Viking remains have been excavated and are now on show in the Jorvik Viking museum.

Tourist Information

British Tourist Authority have an office at the railway station and another in Tower Street, City centre.

Local Transport

The best way to see the sights is to take the Sightseeing Bus. You can get off and on as often as you like.

Accommodation

Deluxe

Royal York, Station Road, YO2 2AA, ph (0904) 653 681 - 145 rooms with bath. Luxury hotel with all facilities next to station. Tourist bus picks up at door. Restaurants, bars. B&B single £85-£100, double £105-£175.

First Class

The Churchill, 65 Bootham, YO3 7DQ, ph (0904) 644 456 - 13 rooms with bath. Comfortable and homely. Restaurant, bar, bar meals. Five minutes walk from town. B&B Single and double £35-£45.

Judges Lodging, 9 Lendal, YO1 2AQ, ph (0904) 638 733 - 12 rooms with bath. Dates from 1700 former home of Assize Court Judges. In town centre. Gourmet restaurant, licensed. B&B single £50, double £70.

Bed & Breakfast

Astoria, 6 Grosvenor Terrace, Bootham YO3 7AG - ph (0904) 659 558 - 14 rooms (some with private facilities), TV, coffee making. Close to restaurants and town. Very friendly, family run. Full breakfast. B&B single £17-£24, double £30-£34.

Jorvik, 50-52 Marygate, Bootham YO3 7BH, ph (0904) 653 511 - 23 bedrooms with bath, TV, tea & coffee making. Restaurant, licensed. Five minutes walk to town. B&B single £23-£30, double £40-£60.

Queen Anne's Guest House, 24 Queen Anne's Road, Bootham YO3 7AA, ph (0904) 629 389 - 5 rooms (2 with private facilities), TV, coffee making, central heating. Five minutes walk to Minster. B&B single £12-£14 double £24-£30.

Food and Drink

You cannot claim to have been to York unless you have sampled Yorkshire pudding, made as only the locals can. The batter is formed into a deep circle with a base and filled with cooked beef and onion gravy.

There are plenty of cafes and other eating houses that serve reasonably priced food. Most restaurants serve good wholesome English food. Tea houses are popular.

Sightseeing

The **Gothic Minster** is the most famous building. It has an 11 tonne bell known as Big Peter which tolls every day at noon. Take the time to look at the soaring columns, the choir screen portraying the kings of England and the rose window which commemorates the marriage of King Henry VII to Elizabeth of

York. Visit the **Chapter House** built in the 13th century.

The narrow streets are full of surprises and are well worth wandering through. **Clifford's Tower** stands perched on a grassy mound. Museums abound. **York Castle, Yorkshire, National Railway, Friargate, Regimental, Bar Convent, the Museum of Automata** and **the York Dungeon,** an animated horror museum. You can walk along the 13th century walls, look at the medieval half wooden shops and houses in the centre of the city called the **Shambles.** York also has the most fashionable shopping centre in the north of England.

Sights Further Afield

Within easy reach and well worth seeing are **The Yorkshire Dales**. Apart from the beauty of the scenery, this is James Herriott country. You will see where the real surgery was, the church where he was married and the TV locations.

Another great tour is to **Castle Howard**. This was the stately home used in the TV series *Brideshead Revisited*. It took from 1699-1759 to build. The state rooms are lavish, the chapel interesting and the costume museum well worth seeing. The grounds are beautiful and time should be made to wander through them. The house is occupied by the Howard family.

Yet another interesting tour is to Bronte Country and **Emmerdale**. On this tour you can watch traditional clogs being made. It will be easy to understand how the countryside inspired Emily Bronte to write *Wuthering Heights*.

The Lake District

The Lake District is a beautiful slice of England. The lakes are separated by rugged hills about 900m, high by English standards. The scenery is soft and has a soothing effect. It's no wonder it was the home of so many poets and writers. To appreciate the area you need to walk but most visitors don't have time for this.

Some of the places which can be viewed from a car or bus are **Grasmere** where the poet William Wordsworth lived from 1799 to 1808 at Dove Cottage. The cottage and an adjoining Wordsworth museum are open to the public. Wordsworth spent the last 17 years of his life at nearby Rydal Mount which is also open to the public. He died in 1850 and was buried in Grasmere churchyard where his grave can be seen.

Windermere is the largest lake in England and also the name of the tourist town that lies on its east bank. It is popular with yachtsmen and boaters. Regular trips around the lake are run by the Iron Steamboat Company.

Wast Water has the most spectacular mountains in the district but is not accessible by road.   **Keswick** has the Fitz Park Museum which has manuscripts and letters written by some of the famous authors who lived and wrote some of their best known works while living in the area. Samuel Coleridge moved here in 1800 and lived at Greta Hall. Other writers whose work is displayed include Robert Southey and John Ruskin. Sir Hugh Walpole wrote his famous *Herries Saga* when living in the district. His works are also on display.

Hawkeshead has the building where Wordsworth went to school open to the public. You can also see Ann Tyson's cottage where Wordsworth stayed when a schoolboy.

Sawrey is where Beatrix Potter lived in a country house at Hill Top. The house, with her original manuscripts and drawings,is open to the public from Easter to the end of October.

Accommodation

Superior
Stakis Lodore Swiss, Barrowdale CA12 5UX, ph (7087) 77 285, fax (7687) 77 343 - 70 rooms with private facilities. Upper end of Derwentwater. Restaurant, bar, pool, squash, tennis. Single £61.50-£79, double £99-£105.

Superior Tourist
Crow Park Hotel, The Heads CA12 5ER, phone (7687) 2208 - 28 rooms with private bath. Between Keswick and Derwentwater. Restaurant, 2 bars, parking. Single £19-£21, double £35-£42.
Keswick Hotel, Station Road, Keswick CA12 4NQ, ph (7687) 72

020 - 66 rooms, parking, dining room. 24km from Penrith station. Single £65, double £75.

Manchester

Manchester is situated on the River Irwell which is linked to the Mersey estuary by the Manchester ship canal, built in 1894. It is a main port and the second biggest commercial city in England with a population of 449,168.

History

Originally it was the Roman fort of Mancuniom. It became the cotton capital of the world in the mid-eighteenth century, although most of the cotton mills are outside the city. Today it is a thriving industrial centre producing chemicals, clothing, printing, publishing, paper, food products, rubber and electrical goods. The new airport is less congested than Heathrow and passengers can take the fast rail link and be in the city in 20 minutes. It is a good starting point for touring the various regional areas of Britain outside of London.

Tourist Information

British Tourist Authority has an office at the railway station.

Local Transport

There are buses and trains to wherever you wish to go. Manchester is not a tourist city and does not cater for them in the usual way.

Accommodation

Superior First Class

Piccadilly, Piccadilly Place, M60 1QR, ph (61) 236-8414, fax (61) 236-1568 - 275 rooms with private bath. Very convenient and less than a kilometre from the station. 2 Restaurants, 3 bars. Single £99-£119, double £119-£129.

Moderate First Class

Britannia, Portland Street, MI 3LA, ph (61) 228-2288, fax (61) 236-9154 - 362 rooms with private bath. Restaurant, night club, bars. Five minutes from station and conveniences. Single £75, double £98.

Sashas, Tib Street, M4 IPQ, ph (61) 228-1234, fax (61) 236-9202 - 223 rooms with facilities. Less than a kilometre from station. Restaurant, bars. Single £25-55, double £30-77.

Food and Drink

There are plenty of places to eat and drink in Manchester, but there are no special dishes that the city can call its own. Check the menus outside restaurants before entering.

Sightseeing

Although it has been transformed into a modern go-ahead city, its Victorian buildings have been undergoing restoration.

Manchester Cathedral built as a church in the 15th century is well worth a visit. Some of the best known features of this city are the *Guardian,* first published in 1821 as the *Manchester Guardian;* The Halle Orchestra; the Grammar School; the Institute of Science and Technology; and the University, all established in the 19th century.

Cricket fans know Manchester from Test Matches played at **Old Trafford** and Soccer fans either love or hate Manchester United. It claims to be the city where the first atom was split; the first passenger railway station was built; the first test-tube baby was born; the first public library was opened; the first British plane was flown; and the first commercial computer was developed. Quite an achievement for what was a village 200 years ago.

Chester

The quaint, old city of Chester stands on the River Dee. Although it is the capital of Cheshire, its population is only 58,436.

History

The Romans built a fortress called Deva where Chester now stands, in 70AD. They used it when they were endeavouring to conquer the north. It was occupied by the 20th Legion for 300 years. Chester was the last town in England to yield to William the Conqueror in 1070, so he repaid the people of the area by confiscating their land. After the Norman conquest, Cheshire was made a palatine - province of a feudal lord - under the Earl of Chester. It had its own parliament but the Earl owned all the land except that belonging to the church. This situation remained until the reign of Henry Vlll.

Cheshire is rich in literary traditions. Raphael Holinshed was the chief author of a history of Britain on which Shakespeare based fourteen of his plays. Charles Lutwidge Dodgson better known as Lewis Carroll, author of *Alice in Wonderland,* was born in a vicarage near Warrington. Elizabeth Gaskell immortalised the village of Knutsford in her book *Cranford.* William Congreve, the Restoration dramatist also lived in the area. Religious figures linked with Chester include hymn writer Bishop Heber and missionary explorer Sir Wilfred Grenfell.

Tourist Information

The British Tourist Authority has an office at the station.

Local Transport

The best way to see Chester is on the Explorer bus. It is a double decker and can be boarded anywhere. Fares can be paid on the bus but you save £1 if you buy it in advance from BTA.

Keep your ticket as this entitles you to another reduction if you take an explorer trip in another city.

Accommodation

Deluxe

Chester Grosvenor, Eastgate Street, CH1 1LT, ph (244) 32-4024, fax (244) 31-3246 - 86 rooms with bath. In city centre. All facilities, gourmet restaurant, brasserie, bar, gym, piano bar. Charge for parking. Single £105-£120, double £160-£180.

Moderate First Class
Abbots Well, Whitchurch Road, Chriostleton CH3 5QL, ph (244) 33-2121, fax (244) 335-287 - 27 rooms with bath. Restaurant, bar, leisure centre, free parking. 3km from station. Single £75-£89, double £89-£99.

Superior Tourist
Forte Posthouse Wexham Road CH4 9DL, ph (244) 68-0111 - 105 rooms with bath. Restaurant, cocktail bar, pool, leisure centre, sauna. 5km from Chester. Single and double £41.50-£55.50.

Food and Drink
There are plenty of restaurants and tea shops plus pubs where you can have a good English meal.

Sightseeing
The main attractions of Chester are its ancient buildings. The **city walls**, built by the Romans and reinforced by the Normans still stand, and, in fact, it is the only British city where the walls are wholly intact. Roman remains visible today are the ruin of an amphitheatre and the foundations of a large Roman building in the cellar of the shop at 28 Northgate Street. On the north and east side of the city, the walls follow the original Roman construction and incorporate their work. The north-eastern medieval tower is called the **King Charles Tower** because Charles l stood there to watch a Civil War battle in 1645.

The narrow streets are called **Rows**. This is because there are rows of half timbered two-tiered shops all in a line and built in the 1200s. If you follow Forgate Street eastwards and take the right fork at the roundabout, just beyond the Engine House pub, you will see an **ecumenical monument**. It marks the spot where Protestant George Marsh was burned to death by the Catholics in 1555. It also commemorates Saint John Plessington who was hanged, drawn and quartered in 1679 by the Protestants. His relics are venerated at the Franciscan church in Chester. Chester has a Cathedral and several churches. It also boasts the smallest racecourse. There is a wharf where you can hire a boat and explore the River Dee.

Sights Further Afield

Chester is close to North Wales and there is a good road along the coast. The model manufacturing village of **Sunshine** built in 1888 is a short distance. William, Lord Leverhulme and his brother James started a soap manufacturing company known to this day as Lever Bros. He introduced profit-sharing, pensions, medical care and other benefits for his employees.

Bath

Bath is a sleepy, quiet city resting on the banks of the River Avon in South West England. It has a population of 84,454.

History

It was discovered by the Romans and named Aquae Sulis because of its mineral springs. The Romans turned it into a spa resort covering six acres with pools reaching temperatures of 49C (120F). They are still intact today. After the Romans left, the Britons neglected the town and even built over some of the spa pools. The Roman baths were rediscovered in 1879.   Bath became fashionable in the 18th century when famous people went there to "take the waters". Dickens, Swinburne, Defoe, Jane Austen and scores of other people of note found the soothing atmosphere conducive to inspiration.

Tourist Information

British Tourist Authority has an office at the railway station.

Local Transport

There are plenty of local buses that will take you to different points in the city, or you can take a tour bus thus ensuring that you will see all the points of interest.

Accommodation

Deluxe

Bath Spa, Sydney Road, BA2 6JF, ph (225) 444-424, fax (225)

444-006, 98 rooms all facilities. Georgian mansion built in 1850, renovated. Parking. Walking distance to all sights. 2 restaurants, bar. Single £125, double £160.

First Class
The Francis, Queen Square, BA1 2HH, ph (225) 42-4257 - 98 rooms with bath. Built in 1729. Overlooking Georgian Square. Between Royal Crescent and the Abbey. Restaurant, bar. Single £88, double £108.

Moderate First Class
Cliff Hotel, Lansdown Grove, Lansdown Road, BA3 6HY, ph (225) 72-3226, fax (225) 72-3871 - 45 rooms with bath. Restaurant, bar. 8km from station. Single £50-£65, double £80-£110.

Food and Drink
There are plenty of cafes and small restaurants, not to mention the pubs where food is served. The only alleged local delicacy is the Bath bun. There is a cafe in North Parade Passage called Sally Lunns where they still bake the bun with the same name.

Sightseeing
The Georgian nobles built elegant houses mostly in sweeping curves. The best example of this distinctive architecture is the **Royal Crescent**, an arc of thirty houses overlooking extensive lawns. House no. 1 is open to the public. No. 15 is the fictional home of Sir Percy Blakeney, the Scarlet Pimpernel. **The Circus**, where the houses are built in a circle is close by. Dr Livingstone lived at no. 13, and the painter Gainsborough at no 17 where he painted the famous *Blue Boy*. As it is uphill, take a bus up to Royal Crescent and walk back.

The ancient attractions are all in the centre of the city.
Next to the Roman baths is the **Pump Room**. Here you can have morning or afternoon tea served as one would imagine it being done in the 18th century. A string quartet plays music by the old masters. Thakeray used the Pump Room as one of the locations in Vanity Fair. The **Roman Baths** are open Mon-Sat 9.30am-5pm. Admission is £5 adult, £3 child.

Bath Abbey, built in the 16th century, is famous for the stone angels who climb ladders to Heaven on the facade. Inside, Australians would be interested in a memorial to Governor Philip who lived just off the Circus at 19 Bennett Street. The house bears a plaque. Don't miss the covered **Pultaney Bridge**.

The **Museum of Costume** which houses original garments since the late 1500s is of interest to everyone not just those with an eye for fashion. The clothes have been well preserved. It is housed in the **Assembly Rooms** frequently mentioned by Jane Austen in her novels of early 19th century life.

Across the Avon in another 18th century building is the **Holbourne Museum** and **Crafts Study Centre**. It has a superb collection of 17th and 18th century art.

Sights Further Afield

For those with the time, a tour to **Longleat**, the home of the Marquise of Bath is worth a visit. The house is the finest example of Elizabethan architecture in the country. Built in 1550 it burnt down in 1567 and was rebuilt in 1572. The house is open all year round. There is also a lion safari park in the grounds.

Edinburgh

The city of Edinburgh is dignified. It is the capital of Scotland and the second largest city, with a population of 419,187. Nowadays it is a cultural centre thanks in the main to the Edinburgh Festival.

History

Strategically placed on the shores of the Firth of Forth, it played an important part in the wars between England and Scotland in medieval times. When James Vl became James l of England and moved his court south, it lost some of its importance. In recent years this has been gained by its contribution to learning.

Tourist Information

Scottish Tourist Board at the railway station.

Local Transport

There are plenty of buses to all parts of the city. In the centre it is better to walk.

Accommodation

Deluxe

George Inter-Continental, 19 George Street, EH2 2PB, ph (31) 225-1251, fax (31) 220-5644 - 195 rooms with all facilities. Close to sightseeing, 200m from castle. Gourmet French restaurant, bars. Single £125, double £150.

Moderate First Class

Friendly Commodore, Cramond Foreshore, EH4 SE1, ph (31) 336-1700, fax (31) 336-4934 - 51 rooms with private bath. On riverside, 8km from airport. Restaurant, bar. Comfortable and friendly like its name. Recently renovated. Single £58-£70, double £72-£85.

Old Waverley, 43 Princes Street, EH2 2BY, ph (31) 556-4668, fax (31) 557-6316 - 66 rooms with bath and facilities. Built in 1848 but has been renovated. Situated over shops opposite the station. It is right in the heart of it all. The hotels boasts a restaurant, bar. Single £76, double £122.

Inexpensive

Terrace Hotel, 37 Royal Terrace, ph (031) 556-3423, fax (031) 556-2520 - Elegant, listed Georgian town house, 15 minutes walk from Princes Street. B&B £19-£30.

Gilmore Guest House, 51 Gilmore Place, EH3 9NT, ph (031) 229-5008 - 6 rooms some with ensuite. B&B £11-£25.

Strathmohr House, 23 Mayfield Gardens, EH9 2BX, ph (031) 667-8694 - 7 rooms with bath, TV, coffee making. B&B £14-£26

Food and Drink

The Scots have a dish called *haggis* which is delicious although some people steer clear of it because of the recipe. It consists of oatmeal, minced offal, suet and seasoning, cooked in maw (stomach of a sheep).

Seafood is one specialty and oyster bars are plentiful. Others are *Scotch whisky, smoked haddock, salmon, kippers, herrings, and cock-a-leekie soup,* which is made from a whole fowl and leeks with other seasonings. *Dunlop cheese* has a rich, mellow flavour. Another very local dish is "tatties an' herrin" (potatoes and herring boiled together).

Shopping

The best buys are tweed materials. Tweed made into garments is very popular and quite unique. Fine woollen items, silk shawls, worsteds and linen are also popular.

Sightseeing

Edinburgh Castle dominates the city. The best view is from Princes Street. Inside you can inspect the apartments occupied by Mary Queen of Scots, including the room where she gave birth to James l. The crown jewels are also kept here. These were recovered by Sir Walter Scott. There is a collection of antique weapons, the banqueting hall and military museum. At 1 pm each day a cannon is fired, a 150 year tradition. Other attractions within the castle are the 11th century St Margaret's Chapel, Old Parliament Hall, and the small cemetery containing the remains of military mascots. There is a changing of the guard ceremony, but it is the antithesis of that at Buckingham Palace, being very relaxed with the participants obviously enjoying themselves.

The National War Memorial stands close by. The **Royal Mile** is a cobbled street lined with interesting shops and houses, including one that was occupied by John Knox in 1560. Below the Castle is a wide parade ground where the Edinburgh Tattoo is held. At the end of the road stands the palace of **Holyrood House**. It is the Queen's official residence but visitors can inspect it when she is not staying there. Inside there are many antiquities including needlework done by Mary Queen of Scots. A plaque commemorates the place where her secretary Rizzio was murdered on the instructions of Queen Mary's husband, Lord Darnley.

There are many small streets running off the Royal Mile.

In **Lawnmarket** stands the six storey tenement house built in 1620, and known as Gladstone's Land. It is furnished in the style of a merchant's house of the time. The ceilings are magnificently painted. Nearby is Lady Stair's House a town dwelling of 1622. It has exhibits by Sir Walter Scott, Robert Louis Stevenson and Robbie Burns. In High Street the Cathedral called **The High Kirk of St Giles** dates from the 12th century.

Canongate was once a separate burgh outside the walls of Edinburgh. **Huntley House**, built in 1520 is a museum featuring Edinburgh's history and social life. The most impressive structure along **Princes Street** is the 60m statue of Sir Walter Scott. Not far away are the National Gallery, Zoological park, Parliament House, Greyfriars Churchyard, the Museum of Childhood and the Royal Scottish Museum.

Sights Further Afield

Three miles from the city is **Craigmillar Castle**. Not far from the city is the ancient seaport and castle of **Dunbar** and the fashionable resort of **North Berwick**.

Glasgow

Glasgow, Strathclyde, on the River Clyde, is the largest city in Scotland and the third largest city in the United Kingdom, with a population of 762,288. It is a relatively modern city with character. Not many buildings pre-date the Victorian era. Its once depressed areas, including the Gorbals, have long been levelled and replaced.

History

Glasgow was an early religious and learning centre in the 12th century. Shipbuilding was always one of its major industries, but it has now declined. Both the *Queen Mary* and the *Queen Elizabeth* were built along the River Clyde. Other industries include engineering, textiles, brewing, chemicals and whisky blending. Glasgow grew rapidly after 1707 when Scotland was united with England. It was the chief port for the importation of tobacco and sugar from the New World.

It survived the industrial revolution with its deposits of coal and iron ore nearby.

Tourist Information
The Sottish Tourist Board has offices in Glasgow.

Local Transport
Buses are plentiful. Tours are also available.

Accommodation

Superior First Class
Glasgow Marriott, 500 Argyle Street, G3 8KK, ph (41) 226-5577, fax (41) 221 9202 - 298 rooms with private bath, and all facilities. Restaurant, bar. 8km from airport with free transport. Less than a kilometre from the city centre. Single & double £110.

Moderate First Class
Jury's Pond, Great Western Road, G12 OX1, ph (41) 334-8161, fax (41) 334-3846 - 137 rooms with private bath. 11km from city centre. Restaurant, bar, health club. Single & double £69.
Stakis Ingram, 201 Ingram Street, GI 1DQ, ph (41) 248-4401, fax (41)226-5149 - 90 rooms with private bath. All facilities. Steakhouse, licensed. In city centre. Single £49.50, double £59.50.

Inexpensive
Hampton Court Hotel, 230 Renfrew Street, ph (041) 332-6623/5885 - 15 rooms. Iron, tea and coffee making, TV, licensed. Evening meal by arrangement. £16-£25.99.
Dunkeld Hotel, 10-12 Queens Drive, ph (041) 424-0160 - 21 rooms, 10 bathrooms. Iron, licensed, TV, basins, coffee making, evening meal by arrangement. £16-£25.99.
Kirklee Hotel, 11 Kensington Gate G12 9LG, ph (041) 248-3458- 5 Rooms, 5 bathrooms. Iron, basins, TV, coffee making. £16-25.99.
Smiths Hotel, 963 Sauchiehall Road, ph (041) 339-6363/7674 - 33 rooms. Iron, basin, TV, tea and coffee making. £16-£25.

Food and Drink
Good wholesome food is readily available. Some restaurants serve continental fare. Seafood, smoked and fresh salmon, haggis are local specialties.

Shopping

Glasgow has one of the finest shopping thoroughfares in Britain, Sauchiehall Street. You can buy almost anything here.

Sightseeing

St Munro's Cathedral dates from the 12th century. Glasgow University was built in 1451. Other places of interest are: **Kelvingrove Art Gallery and Museum** houses a fine collection of European art including Salvador Dali's famous painting of the Crucifixion. The **Museum of Transport** includes a re-creation of a 1938 street. The **Glasgow School of Art** was designed by Charles Rennie Mackintosh and contains much of his work. The **Burrell Art Collection** is housed in a gallery in Pollock Park.

Glasgow also has the biggest football stadium in Britain, **Hampden Park**. In 1989, at **Culcreuch Castle**, a short distance north of Glasgow, *Tom Moody*, an Australian cricketer, won a haggis-throwing competition with a throw of 67m, beating the local record of 50m.

Sights Further Afield

A short distance from Glasgow are some of the most scenic areas in the whole of Scotland. **Loch Lomond**, is one of the most beautiful lakes in Europe. It can be reached in less than an hour. Trips are usually extended into the loch and mountainous country of **Argyle**. The road takes you through the charming little town of **Inveraray** where the Duke of Argyle, Chief of the Clan Campbell has his castle.

On the Atlantic side of Glasgow, the sea-lochs cleave deep into the mountains. The wild scenery of **Loch Long**, one of the longest, deepest and most beautiful fjords is easily accessible. Charming **Loch Goil** is right on Glasgow's doorstep.

Belfast

The Capital of Northern Ireland is situated on the banks of the River Lagan, where it flows into the Belfast Lough on the border of Counties Antrim and Down. It has a population of 400,000.

History

Belfast became a city in 1888. Surrounding hills are soft and green so typical of the scenery of Northern Ireland. Being a seaport, shipbuilding has always been its main industry, but in modern times electronics and engineering have flourished.

Local Transport

Local public transport is good. Ask at your hotel or the local tourist agency.

Accommodation

Superior First Class

Europa, Great Victoria Street, BT2 7AP, ph (232) 327 000, fax (232) 327 800, 198 rooms with private bath. Central. Gourmet restaurant, pub. Single £45 double £115.

Moderate First Class

Plaza, 15 Brunswick Street, BT2 TGE, ph (232) 333 555, fax (232) 232 999 - 23 rooms, private facilities. This hotel was completely renovated in 1992. Quiet part of centre, five minutes from station and Cathedral. Single £35-£59, double £45-£69.

Dukes, 65 University Street, BT7 1HL, ph (232) 236 666, fax (232) 237 177 - 21 rooms with bath. Part of the Queens University near Botanical Gardens. Two restaurants and three bars, gym and sauna. Single £35-£69, double £45-£79.

Guest Houses

Somerton, 22 Lansdown Road, Phone (0232) 370 717 - 8 rooms. £15-£20. *Lismore Lodge*, 410 Ormeau Street, ph (0232) 641 205 - 7 rooms. £15-£20. *Ashberry Cottage*, 19 Rosepark Central, Dundonald, ph (0232) 482 441 - 3 rooms. £12-£20.

Food and Drink

Main restaurants offer continental and British specialties but the Irish prefer plain hearty meals of meat, bread and vegetables. Fish and chips and home baked bread made from whole-wheat flour are specialities. Try the pubs for a good meal at a reasonable price.

Shopping

Best buys are Belfast linen and Irish whiskey.

Men's shirts and collars made in Londonderry are world renowned for their quality.

Sightseeing

The city centre is dominated by the dome of the **City Hall**. This building is topped by **Cave Hill** from where, on a clear day, you can see the Isle of Man and the Ayreshire coast. Parliament met in Belfast from 1921-1972 then moved to **Stormont**, five miles outside the city. The dignified building, where it now meets, is made of Portland stone and was opened in 1932 by the then Prince of Wales. Nearby is the Prime Minister's House.

The **Queen's University** received a Royal Charter in 1909. For those who like museums the **Ulster Folk and Transport Museum** consists of farmhouses, watermills, a whole village, shops and church, all moved from the countryside. **Mount Stewart House and Gardens** are rated by the National Trust in the top six in the UK. Ulster Museum, Palm House and Tropical Ravine are all in Belfast's **Botanical Gardens**. The Palm House was begun in 1839.

Belfast Zoo offers a wonderful view of the city and lough. Along the north bank of Belfast Lough stands a small community called **Carrickfergus**. Here the ancestors of Andrew Jackson, President of the USA, kept an inn. On the waterfront stands an inscribed stone to commemorate the landing of King William lll who was on his way to defeat James l at the Battle of the Boyne. Within sight of Carrickfergus' ancient castle and in the Belfast Lough, Captain John Paul Jones, a Scottish gardener ran up his colours on the *Ranger* and fought it out with HMS *Drake*. He was one of the founders of the US Navy.

Sights Further Afield

One of the most picturesque and scenic highways in Europe is a winding road running north from Belfast along the coast. At times the road is so close to the water that the windscreen is covered with spray. The highway crosses rocky peninsulas with views of basalt highlands and the deep waters of the Irish Sea. Well worth the time.

Index

Photographs

Where captions do not appear in the text.

Facing Inside Front Cover: Repairing a Fountain, Villa Borguese, Rome

Facing page 17: A street in Salzburg

Facing page 48: Parliament, Vienna

Facing page 49: Partial view of Nice

Facing page 112: Vatican Apartments that overlook the Square

Facing page 113: Carabinieri (local police) in Rome

Facing page 129: Windsor Castle, United Kingdom

Inside Back Cover: Museo dell' Opera del Duomo, Florence